3

Contents

Dedication 7
Preface 9

PART ONE – *Beginnings*

Chapter One – *Meet Marian* 13
Chapter Two – *Bihar* 17
Chapter Three – *The Indian Trains* 23
Chapter Four – *Meet Calvin* 27
Chapter Five – *Missionary Appointment* 31
Chapter Six – *Rendezvous* .35
Chapter Seven – *The Wedding* 41
Chapter Eight – *Pakistan* 45
Chapter Nine – *The Religion of Islam* 47
Chapter Ten – *A Woman's Role in Muslim
   Society* 49
Chapter Eleven – *Bengali-A Poetical
   Language* 55
Chapter Twelve – *Rest and Relief* 59
Pictures 63

PART TWO – *Gopalganj and Village Life*

Chapter Thirteen – *Gopalganj* 69
Chapter Fourteen – *The Village House* 73
Chapter Fifteen – *Village Culture* 79
Chapter Sixteen – *The Postman Doesn't Knock* 81
Chapter Seventeen – *The Dying Dead* 83
Chapter Eighteen – *Village Churches* 87
Chapter Nineteen – *The Big Day* 91
Chapter Twenty – *Convention-Village Style* 95

4

Chapter Twenty-One – *Storms, Floods, and Riots* 101
Chapter Twenty-Two – *Travel* 107
Chapter Twenty-Three – *Bridges and Gangplanks* .111
Chapter Twenty-Four – *Foot Paths* 115
Chapter Twenty-Five – *Rest Rooms and I* 119
Chapter Twenty-Six – *Miracles* 125
Chapter Twenty-Seven – *Demons* 129
Chapter Twenty-Eight – *Cholera Epidemic-1964* . . .133
Pictures 137

PART THREE – *Dhaka*

Chapter Twenty-Nine – *A Church Is Born* 145
Chapter Thirty – *New Assignment* 149
Chapter Thirty-One – *The Bug...Twice Bought* 153
Chapter Thirty-Two – *Eviction* 157
Chapter Thirty-Three – *New Location* 161
Chapter Thirty-Four – *Hospitality* 163
Chapter Thirty-Five – *Early Believers* 167
Chapter Thirty-Six – *Miracles of Healing* 171
Chapter Thirty-Seven – *God's Strategy* 175
Chapter Thirty-Eight – *Poverty* 179
Chapter Thirty-Nine – *Rickshaws* 183
Chapter Forty – *Dilu Road* 187
Chapter Forty-One – *Education* 191
Chapter Forty-Two – *Black Thursday* 193
Chapter Forty-Three – *A Nation Splits* 197
Chapter Forty-Four – *Civil War* 199
Chapter Forty-Five – *Terrorists* 203
Chapter Forty-Six – *India Enters the War* 205
Chapter Forty-Seven – *The Rescue* 207
Chapter Forty-Eight – *Rebuilding a Nation* 209

Bangladesh,
Tears
and
Laughter

By Marian Olson

বাংলাদেশ   BANGLADESH

Chapter Forty-Nine – *Guarding the Land* 211
Chapter Fifty – *Purchasing Land* 215
Chapter Fifty-One – *The Impossible* 217
Chapter Fifty-Two – *Interventions* 221
Chapter Fifty-Three – *Financing the Project* 223
Chapter Fifty-Four – *Lost Records* 227
Pictures 231

PART FOUR – *Cal's Wife*

Chapter Fifty-Five – *Adjustments* 239
Chapter Fifty-Six – *Germ Warfare* 243
Chapter Fifty-Seven – *I Lost My Kitchen* 247
Chapter Fifty-Eight – *Order or Convenience* 251
Chapter Fifty-Nine – *Emotional Strains* 253
Chapter Sixty – *Cultural Conflicts* 257
Chapter Sixty-One – *In Sickness* 261
Chapter Sixty-Two – *Furlough Adjustments* 265
Chapter Sixty-Three – *We Are Different* 269
Chapter Sixty-Four – *Where Are Your Children?* . . .273
Chapter Sixty-Five – *God Gave Us Family* 277
Chapter Sixty-Six – *My Neighbor Judy* 281
Chapter Sixty-Seven – *Tara* 283
Chapter Sixty-Eight – *Christa Egli* 287
Pictures 291

PART FIVE – *The Man I Married*

Chapter Sixty-Nine – *Calvin, the Man* 297
Chapter Seventy – *Servanthood* 301
Chapter Seventy-One – *Physical Weakness* 303
Chapter Seventy-Two – *Confused Guidance* 305
Chapter Seventy-Three – *Fasting* 307

6

Chapter Seventy-Four – *As a Spiritual Father* 311
Chapter Seventy-Five – *Asa* .315
Chapter Seventy-Six – *A Difficult Change* 317
Chapter Seventy-Seven – *Fasting for Albania* 319
Chapter Seventy-Eight – *Bangladesh –
   The Now Country* 323
Chapter Seventy-Nine – *The Last Days* 325
Chapter Eighty – *Promotion* 329
Pictures 335

Epilogue 341

Dedication

This book is dedicated to our parents, siblings, colleagues, and friends worldwide who supported our ministry with prayer and finances, and to the people of Bangladesh who enriched our lives.

Appreciation is due each one who encouraged me to write these memoirs, and to Phil and Julie Parshall, Stan and Ann Steward, and Mark Peterson who assisted in the final editing. Appreciation is also due to Char Dykstra for layout and typesetting, and to Ron Baker for the cover artwork.

Preface

In more than 30 years of missionary service, no one has played a greater role in forming me as a missionary than Calvin and Marian Olson. In fact, without their intervention, I doubt if we would be in missions today. God chose to use them to draw our attention to the needs of the world. Calvin and Marian were there as we listened to God's voice and call into missions.

Calvin and Marian were at the airport in Dhaka when we first arrived in the country. We lived in their home for the first five weeks and prayed together for God's wisdom and direction in one of the most needy areas of the world. I know the Olsons better than I know my own family members. They are for real. Their dedication, commitment, love for lost people, and prayer life are legendary.

Wherever I go in the world people will often ask, "Do you know the Olsons?" The impact of their lives goes far beyond the borders of India and Bangladesh. I commend this book to you. You are about to take a wonderful journey into the lives of two of God's choice servants. I have been blessed to have them as friends and mentors. May God speak also to your heart as you read their adventures.

Jerry L. Parsley
Assemblies of God
Regional Director for Eurasia

Marian went to India in 1950 as a single missionary. There she met her future husband, Calvin Olson, from Minnesota. The story of their romance, marriage, and ministry has spanned a half century. War, famine, floods, disease, and danger were frequent companions of the Olsons. They faced daunting obstacles with courage and serenity, never wavering in their love for the people of Bangladesh and India.

Calvin's exemplary life and spiritual leadership endeared him to millions. Marian's beautiful, optimistic, steadfast spirit and her abandonment to the call of God brought respect to her husband and their ministry. Throughout Bangladesh, India, and America thousands of believers and fellow ministers have been encouraged and strengthened by the Olson's life and ministry.

I first met Calvin and Marian Olson thirty-two years ago in Dhaka, Bangladesh. For over three decades my life has been enriched by the friendship of this godly missionary couple. Since Calvin's home-going to Glory in March 2000, his life and ministry continue to speak encouragement to us.

It is an honor for me to recommend this book of the life and ministry of Calvin and Marian Olson. I speak on behalf of hundreds of missionary colleagues and national leaders who have been eternally blessed and encouraged by this couple. This book is Marian's gift not only to Calvin but also to all of us who share their passion for missions. It is my prayer that the generations to come will be blessed by the testimony of this marvelous missionary couple.

David Grant
Southern Asia Area Director
Assemblies of God World Missions

PART ONE
Now in the Beginning...

"Two shall be born the whole wide world apart and speak in different tongues,
   And have no thought each of the other's being, and no heed.
   Yet these o'er unknown seas to unknown lands shall cross, escaping wreck,
   Defying death and all unconsciously shape every act
   And bend each wandering step to this one end that someday out of darkness
   They shall meet and read life's meaning in each other's eyes...."

–Author Unknown

Chapter One

We knew we were watched. He waved to us as we drove out of our lane. He sometimes stopped by for a cup of tea and a new ballpoint pen. Once he just happened to be eating at the same restaurant that we were eating at. We recognized him in the audience during a Sunday church meeting.

One day he delivered a letter to us with a government seal, dated March 1998. "Calvin P. and Marian N. Olson are hereby requested to leave the Republic of Bangladesh within seven days. Report to our office with passport for necessary stamp of travel permit."

We both had celebrated our 65th birthdays and had served 35 years in Bangladesh.

Meet Marian
"And God Made a Woman"

On Ocracoke Island of the Outer Banks of North Carolina, in the home of paternal grandparents, the midwife handed a nine pound infant girl, the second child, to Almyrta and William Midgett. They named her

Marian Naomi. It was October 24, 1924. Grandfather William Thomas Midgett, light house keeper, was on duty that night.

A few years later our family moved to Wilmington, Delaware where I, along with three sisters and two brothers, spent most of my preadult years.

A neighbor known as "Aunty Gordon" served as baby sitter to five children while my mother was hospitalized with child number six in May 1934. Aunty took me to Sunday School at an Assembly of God Church where at age ten I placed my faith in Jesus. It wasn't long before my entire family began attending the church and a Christian home was established.

At an early age I understood that one day I would be a missionary. Though the teen years were filled with other dreams, that "call" to serve God in a foreign country never left me.

After completing studies at Eastern Bible Institute, later renamed Valley Forge Christian College, I applied for a missionary appointment. My application was rejected because I was not married. The mission board advised me to take nurses training. After completing my nurses training in New York City, I reapplied for a second time only to be rejected again as there was still no vacancy for a single lady.

I then served a year as an inner city missionary for Bethel Church in Newark, New Jersey, after which I applied the third time and was accepted in the summer of 1950. My home church, First Assembly of God of Wilmington, Delaware, pledged eighty dollars monthly support which made up my total budget.

In November 1950 I set sail with eleven other passengers, on the "City of Swansea," a British freighter headed for India. After six weeks the vessel arrived in

Calcutta on Christmas day. Traumatized by the poverty, odors, and foreign language, I had the added discomfort of not seeing another white face. No one had come to receive me. With no local currency and only an address I hired a taxi, which, to the amazement of all, delivered me to the right place.

The following day I was escorted twenty four hours by train northward to Bihar Province where I would serve for five years in an orphanage and school for girls.

Chapter Two

Bihar
"The Garden of India "

I traveled from village to village in a predominantly
Hindu community with two Indian ladies who were
Christian. We rode over the rough dirt roads sitting on
the flat boards of a horse cart with our legs dangling
over the side. This was during a season called "Loo"
when the winds from the desert in the west blew
through our province kicking up the dust to resemble a
snow storm. When we arrived at our destination either
by cart or car we were completely covered with dust.
We could even taste it.

As a white skinned, blue eyed American, I stood out
in a crowd. The people were curious to see me, to
touch me, and to hear my strange language. I was often
surrounded by dark-skinned, black-haired children with
large black eyes, who just "came to see."

On one occasion, in the cool season, when I was
wearing nylon hose I suddenly felt something touch my
leg. I had learned enough of the Hindi language by then
to understand their whispering chatter. They wanted to
know why my legs and arms were not the same color?
Some brave child ventured to pull at my stocking to
prove a point. It struck me as funny so I laughed with

them.

In time I was prodded with questions, "Why did you come to my country? Why did you leave your father and mother. Don't you love them? Why aren't you married? Couldn't your father afford a wedding?" I would always be an oddity.

Tugging at my arm one woman invited me into her house. She bowed low, touching my feet in the traditional greeting saying, "I like to touch your skin. It is so soft. Here, you can hold my baby. You can be her mother." She ran her rough dirty fingers through my hair. She lifted my dress to see what I wore underneath. "So white you are. Are you sick? I like you." And I became her friend.

One day an aged Hindu woman, who was only as tall as my shoulder, came to me with many questions. Though she had spent her life worshipping many gods, she eventually placed her faith in Christ. Even though she lived in poverty her face now shone with joy and hope.

She lived in a one room house with a mud floor and a grass roof. She owned only one change of clothing, one cooking pot, a brass plate, a can to drink from, a clay stove, an oil lamp, and a low stool for visitors.

Looking into my eyes she uttered these words. "We are poor now, in Heaven we will be rich. We are hungry in this world, in Heaven we will have too much food. We wear rags here, in Heaven we will wear beautiful clothes. I want to go to heaven. You told me how to get ready. We have nothing to give you but our house is yours. Can't you stay with us?"

Walking through a village on one occasion I suddenly stopped. There before me was a manger scene illuminated by the morning sun. Wrapped in a dusty white cloth the newborn baby lay on a pile of straw in a hand woven basket resting on the sunbaked mud floor. The mother, clothed in a sari, squatted beside her child, shielding the little one from the sun's rays. In the background stood a newborn calf on wobbling legs. The mother was honored to have me take her picture.

Followers of the Hindu religion consider the cow to be holy and can think of nothing better than to be born as a cow in the next life. Cows wander where and when they please. In Calcutta City I saw them lying on the steps of a modern bank building. Busy traffic winds its way around the ambling cows.

The droppings from the cow are plastered on wounds as healing ointment or mixed with straw and dried in cakes to be used as fuel to cook the daily meal. I once saw a mother whose baby was suffering from an earache, lift her baby into the flow of urine from a cow. The mother was sure her baby would find relief from this holy liquid.

The daily trip to the village well became an anticipated social visit with other women. As the clear tube well water flowed slowly into their large clay pots the women exchanged gossip. There would be the latest news of an upcoming wedding, the death of a family member or the purchase of a cow or goat. Within twenty minutes they were on their way again, baby on one hip and a five gallon jug of water on the other.

Who can say what transpired in their hearts as I squatted before their low mud stoves watching the boiling pots of rice, holding their babies in my lap, speaking their language, and answering questions they could ask no one else.

How much of God could they see in the hands that delivered their babies, washed their children's wounds, and gave injections to the whole community during a cholera epidemic. Love had to shine through, and love wins.

They not only gave me many cups of hot tea cooked with milk and sugar, but they taught me by example the joy of a simple lifestyle and hospitality. The trips to the villages to share the Gospel were beyond my expectations.

Second year language exams behind me I joined an evangelism group heading for a remote area on the border of Nepal via a jungle. There were four singles and two couples that made up our party. The ages ranged from 16 (son of Norwegian missionaries) to 45 years.

Our caravan had to travel by jeep on an ox cart road, through a large wooded area where no four wheel vehicle had ever gone. In some places with pick and ax we had to make our own road.

What was to be a day's trip turned into two as our

jeep, one of two vehicles, broke down on the edge of the jungle at dusk. It meant camping there for the night. The ladies slept inside the vehicles while the men slept in a tent with one standing guard duty. The evening meal was cooked over a hole in the ground with twigs and leaves as fuel. It could have been romantic and enjoyable had there not been the fear of wild animals.

The following day we resumed our journey until we reached a clearing in a grove of trees just outside a village. There we set up camp with five tents arranged in a circle. In the center would be a large bonfire which would burn all night to ward off the bears. By day we traveled in pairs to the surrounding villages with printed literature in hand, looking for opportunities to share the Gospel.

Sitting around the fire at night we shared the day's experiences. We learned a Hindu holy man (sadhu) had shown great interest. On the last day of our tour this holy man accepted water baptism in a large mud hole. We can only believe that he, like Paul of the New Testament, led his own people to the only true God.

As we broke camp we heard gun shots in the distance. Not long after we saw Paul Schoonmaker, one of our team, triumphantly dragging a bear into camp. This was my initiation into missionary life.

Chapter Three

The Indian Trains
*"Missed your train? Don't worry,
there will be another one tomorrow."*

My first train trip alone in India was one never to
be forgotten. The trains differ from our western
trains as the compartments are not joined. You cannot
walk from one to another. You entered the
compartment from the station platform and exited the
same way.

Each train car has it's own cubicle with toilet and
mini basin which usually provides rusty water. There
were two bunk beds with an aisle between. During the
day everyone sat on the lower bunks. At night the
upper decks were used as beds.

You could travel first, second, or third class, or "ladies
only." I was forewarned that traveling with ladies and
small children meant sitting up all night for it would be
very crowded. The men always put all the luggage in
with the women.

On one trip, at the age of 27 and unmarried, I entered
a second class compartment with no passengers. This
meant that once the train left the station I could lock
the door and be alone. Just before the whistle blew a
man came running and jumped into the compartment

with me.

Knowing I would have to share this space with a strange man for 24 hours, I became very uncomfortable. We did not talk to each other but after some observation I decided this well dressed Indian was a gentleman and I had no fears. We would sleep on the two lower bunks with a narrow aisle separating us

In the middle of the night I heard a thud and instantly I was awake. Opening my eyes I discovered my traveling companion had fallen off the bunk onto the floor. As he sat on the bunk to get his bearings I pretended I was still sleeping but had much trouble controlling the urge to laugh.

Another such trip did not turn out so well. I had to disembark from one train, cross over a large river by ferry and board a second train. I chose an empty compartment and locked the door. Anyone wanting to join me would have to pass my scrutiny first.

The station was crowded and I noticed a group of rowdy university men students heading my way. They wanted to join me. I insisted that this was for ladies only. Angry, they began to bang on the door and windows. Fortunately there were bars along with shutters on the windows but the door was not so secure. My heart beat its fastest just before the whistle blew and the train began to move. I'm sure the students found refuge in another compartment and fortunately I did not see them again.

Years later after I had married, for some reason Calvin

and I could not travel in the same compartment. At the last moment I was pushed inside with a crowd of ladies. During the rocking trip over the rails, our bodies juggling against each other, I felt a hand touch mine. The lady next to me was completely veiled. We had not attempted any conversation. Thinking she wanted to be friendly I did not withdraw my hand. Often women and children liked to touch my white skin so I thought little of it.

It wasn't long before I felt both hands at work on my ring finger. Could it be she was after my wedding rings? I suddenly withdrew my hand and pretended nothing had happened. If she had succeeded in taking my rings no one would have believed my story, and no one would have dared lift her veil to prove it.

I have never been so thirsty and so dirty as on such train trips. Windows are left open for circulation of air. Coal was used to fire the engines and the dust rained havoc on it's passengers. One of the first things your hostess did when you arrived at her home was to offer you a cool drink and show you the bath tub. How refreshing! I tried that with a guest in America once and got an entirely different response.

Due to exposure to the tropical climate, change of food and Southern Asia "bugs" I soon developed intestinal problems which would never entirely leave me for fifty years. While still in language school in Landour Mussoorie, my first year in India, I was hospitalized for minor surgery. During the next three years I would have two more surgeries; one in Calcutta and the other in KVellore, South India. Having been healthy all my life I found this frustrating. Somehow, I was able to continue serving in the orphanage and by the fourth year the problem was under control.

Chapter Four

Meet Calvin
"God Created a Man"

Florence, daughter of Norwegian parents, P. C. and Mrs. Peterson of Willmar, Minnesota, and Sam Olson, son of immigrants from Norway, married and had three sons. Calvin Philip, the middle son, was born April 16, 1924

Calvin's father, a photographer, captured much of those early years with his camera: Calvin crying over a broken toy truck; as a four year old sitting on the front steps of the family home with an open book moving his lips as though preaching; picnics with the family at Green Lake; Cal in his band uniform posing with his cornet; sitting in front of the Christmas tree with brothers James and Gordon; lounging on the bank of a creek with fishing gear; and batting the tennis ball against the wall of the garage, practicing serves.

Calvin also enjoyed sharing glimpses of his childhood which were not photographed. One day he was peddling home from the grocery store with a loaf of bread clamped behind the cycle seat when he suddenly noticed a trail of bread slices behind him and an empty wrapper flapping in the breeze.

At the age of 14, he joined two friends skating on "stink canal," a drainage ditch, in below zero weather.

The ice gave way and one of his friends fell into the freezing water. He was quickly pulled to safety and a fire was built on the bank to thaw out the stiff clothing.

One of his favorite sports as a child was trapping gophers with neighborhood boys. The little animals would stick their heads out of their holes right into a waiting noose that Calvin and his friends had planted.

One of his daring acts was swinging from limb to limb in the trees in the yard using his hands, in full view of his petrified mother staring out the kitchen window.

After the wedding of friends he told of chasing the bride and groom through the streets of Willmar which ended in "someone" getting a ticket.

At the early age of ten he experienced a "spiritual birth." His focus in life was changed. He became very sensitive to right and wrong, and he desired to please God. This took place while attending Sunday School in a one room school house two miles south of Willmar. There he began his spiritual journey which would eventually lead him to Bangladesh as a missionary.

After one year of college he was drafted into the U.S. Navy. He served for three years in the South Pacific during World War II as a radio man. Calvin tells of every ship in his fleet being torpedoed except the one he was assigned to. He watched a burial ceremony as twelve men were lowered into the sea. Kneeling on the deck of the ship he recommitted his life to serving God as a minister and missionary-a vow which he kept till his death.

Returning to college he graduated in 1949 from North Central Bible School. Today it is known as North Central University in Minneapolis, Minnesota. Prior to marriage he co-founded and pastored the Assembly of God Church in Stillwater, Minnesota, for six years.

Working in a grocery store he was able to pay rent on a building used for the congregation. He lived in the basement of that building. Calvin survived on canned baked beans, bread, and discarded produce from the store.

For several years he preached to an audience of five, not counting the visiting students from the college. Today there is a new church building and a healthy congregation in that town.

Chapter Five

Missionary Appointment
"Missionary, A man of God who decodes the message of God and delivers it in the language of earth."
–A. W Tozer

In response to a growing awareness of world missions Calvin sensed an attraction to Southern Asia. Eventually he applied for appointment as missionary to East Pakistan (which later would be renamed Bangladesh). Driving to Springfield, Missouri, for fourteen hours in 100 degree temperatures with no air conditioning in his car, he arrived completely exhausted.

During the interview with the Missions Committee, they observed he was underweight and appeared run down and stressed out. They requested that he have another physical examination and reapply. He eventually received an appointment and proceeded to make preparation for the great move.

Raising money for support and fare was not going to be easy. He took a lot of harassment from colleagues who would have liked to have chosen a mate for him. Leaving New York harbor on a British freighter in August 1954, he began his missionary career, still unmarried.

On his way to East Pakistan the ship stopped in Bombay, India. There Calvin received a telegram from Sydney Bryant, Chairman of the Assemblies of God Missionary Fellowship of North India. He invited Calvin to disembark at once and attend their annual conference. This was a day and night trip by Indian train to Landour Mussoorie, which is situated in the foot hills of the Himalayan mountains at an altitude of about 7000 feet.

At first he hesitated, for at the last minute in New York, he was told that a large trunk had been loaded onto the ship for a missionary in South India. Calvin was responsible for delivering the trunk to our mission office in Calcutta which was the ship's destination. Inquiring of the captain he was assured that no such trunk was on board and if it were they would see that it was off loaded and delivered. The captain was glad to bid farewell to all passengers as the ship was carrying sulfur to be unloaded at Bombay.

Leaving the ship which had been his home for six weeks, Calvin found himself on the streets of Bombay. He knew no one, had no local currency, and spoke only English. It was a holiday and business offices were closed. Somehow he procured the name of a missionary.

He left all his luggage at the train station with a hired coolie to guard it. Hiring a taxi with a name and address they traveled for two hours trying to locate their only hope for help. Finally they arrived unannounced on the couple's door step.

The gentleman could not recommend a hotel, banks were closed so dollar exchange for local currency was not available. They had no guest room and no place to store so much luggage over night.

The wife in the background listening to the conversation interrupted with a suggestion. They could park their car in the driveway and thus make room for Calvin's luggage in the garage. Somehow they could accommodate him for the night and see that he got on his way the next day.

Since all the luggage was at the train station it meant a return trip by taxi to claim it. They found the coolie asleep on top of the pile of suitcases and boxes, including a cornet and typewriter. Nothing was missing.

Chapter Six

Rendezvous
*"So rarely do I find two souls in union
who want only my will and only to serve me."*
–Unknown

Having left the ship early, Calvin purchased a ticket and with limited Indian currency, began the two day trip by train and bus to Landour, Mussoorie, situated in the foothills of the Himalayan mountains. There he would attend a conference for about one hundred Assembly of God missionaries, one third of which were unmarried ladies.

On the second day of the conference he noticed a young lady he had not seen the previous day. He thought perhaps she was a visitor from another mission. He soon discovered that her name was Marian and that she was in charge of the music for the conference as she included him and his cornet on the program.

He noticed that every time he looked my way I was looking at him. Love has a way of entering the heart through the eyes. On the third day an A.G. associate, Irish missionary, David McKee, approached Calvin with, "You are going to East Pakistan, an underdeveloped area of South Asia and living alone will be very difficult in a

Muslim country. I suggest you choose someone from this fine group here. Have you been looking at Marian? We highly recommend her."

Knowing how difficult it would be to talk to a single lady in Indian culture he asked if Calvin would be willing to write to me. He and his wife, Berti, had met and recently married in India so they knew how awkward it was to be single in Asia. But the cultural rules would make getting acquainted difficult. Calvin said he hesitated to speak to any of the single ladies but agreed to write me a letter.

Immediately David made a point to talk with me and asked if I would be willing to correspond with Calvin who had a three month visa for India and would remain in the city of Lucknow to begin language study. I agreed.

One day during coffee break at the conference, Calvin ventured over to the chair where I had been sitting and picked up my Bible. Leafing through it he observed all the markings and notes and said to himself, "Hmm, she'll pass!" We had no conversation during the whole conference but on the last day, along with many others, I shook hands with him, the new missionary.

The first letter arrived five days after I had returned to Bettiah, Bihar, where I served in a girls school and orphanage. Later I learned that Calvin stayed awake all night praying for the Lord's guidance before writing the first letter. He said he got a "green light."

Calvin enjoyed telling this apocryphal account. He arrived in India, heard about a certain young lady, just happened to have her phone number and decided to contact her. After hearing a voice he made sure it was Marian and then asked, "Will you marry me"? There was a moment's hesitation, then came the reply with excitement, "Yes, who's calling."

Calvin had settled for three months in Lucknow to begin studying the Bengali language. Mark Buntain who was to be the speaker for the upcoming tent meeting in that city, suddenly returned to Canada to the bedside of his dying father. The substitute speaker was David McKee, our mediator, who immediately telegraphed me to come as soloist.

By this time Calvin and I had exchanged about three letters. Excitement was high as I anticipated meeting and talking with him. When I arrived, after a 20 hour train trip, there was no one to greet me. I waited a half hour on the station platform searching for a white face.

Meanwhile Calvin, who was staying in a missionary home, asked if any one had been designated to meet Marian at the train station. Yes, the senior missionary, Edgar Barrick, in whose home she would stay, was planning to meet her. Again a question as to what would happen if he forgot. Finally Calvin's host, highly suspicious, agreed to go get her. Calvin offered to go along just to see the city.

There they found me with my suitcase staring into space. Calvin jumped out of the car, shook my hand and reached for my suitcase just as senior missionary Barrick drove up in a cloud of dust. The suitcase and I went into the senior's car.

During the two week tent meetings, Calvin and I sat on opposite ends of the platform, he with his cornet and I with my accordion. Except for the letters, we still had not communicated other than to say hello.

My thirtieth birthday was special. As I left the platform one evening to place my accordion in it's case I saw an envelope which contained birthday greetings and a silver filigree broach from Calvin. Still no words were exchanged.

Gathering up courage he asked the senior missionary if he could take me out to a restaurant to eat. The response was immediate and negative. "In India people don't date. Everyone knows you are not married and many see you on the platform in the tent meetings." So Calvin invited the whole evangelistic party of eight to dinner that night and we got to sit opposite each other for our first conversation.

Knowing how difficult it was for us to get acquainted, our friend and evangelist, David, suggested we ride in the jeep with him and another missionary who were going hunting in a nearby jungle. The traditional American Thanksgiving Day would soon arrive and wild peacock would take the place of turkey for the feast. We agreed to this arrangement. After arriving in the jungle, the two men with their guns ran ahead, following the call of peacocks.

For the first time we were alone. It was then Calvin asked the big expected question. He was quick to add, "Marian, you can never have first place in my life." Since I too had made a commitment years ago to give God first place I found it easy to agree. The first embrace was witnessed by a little dark-skinned, brown-eyed boy of ten peaking through the bushes.

One week later sitting in the living room of a missionary's home we discussed marriage. We had no traditional courtship but we did have an engagement party. While we were celebrating with about ten others, a telegram arrived from the Division of Foreign Missions in the U.S.A., a reply to our request to marry within three months. The reply was negative.

A letter followed, the words of which I include here. "You must wait one year. There is a rule on the books which until now has not been enforced. We will start with you. 'Any single missionary on the field must complete the first year language exam before getting married.'" I qualified but Calvin did not. One other factor was my poor health during the first three years in India. Would I be able to endure the rugged life of Bangladesh?

Chapter Seven

The Wedding
"Many people will walk in and out of your life, but only a true friend will leave foot prints in your heart."
–Eleanor Roosevelt

After our engagement Calvin proceeded to East Pakistan and I remained in India for the next nine months. We could only communicate by letters. There he lived with Orville and Yvonne Carlson and their three preschool children, Renee, Randy, and Rita. He was introduced to the customs of the people, learned to leave his shoes outside, sit cross legged on the floor, and eat rice and curried foods with his fingers.

Immediately he began studying Bengali, one of the most difficult languages of the world. Due to the tropical heat of 100 degrees and living in a house with a tin roof and no electricity (and thus no fans or air conditioning) he lost weight.

Calvin arrived back in India one day before the wedding. Not having seen him for nine months I was not prepared for the skinny frame with kinky curly hair and red mustache which stepped off the train in that little village. This was not the well groomed man in shirt and tie that I had met at a conference. He did agree to shave off the mustache and of course wear a coat and tie for the ceremony.

It rained on the morning of the wedding leaving little puddles on the dirt path from the mission house to the chapel for the 8 a.m. ceremony. It mattered little that the gown of lace had a mud fringe, nor that the soloist had not arrived in time to sing.

The wedding cake which traveled twenty-two hours by train with a guest had naked Cupids holding up each layer. These quickly had to be scraped off and replaced with white ribbon to adjust to the culture.

This was the first western wedding two hundred girls in the orphanage had ever seen. A tea was served under a tent on the lawn in 100 degree temperature. My body was so moist the buttons on my gown rusted by the end of the day.

After eight hours in my wedding gown I changed into traveling clothes for the 22 hour train trip. The first two hours we traveled in a compartment with three single missionary ladies who had attended our wedding. We still had not exchanged a kiss. Weary, covered with soot, and still getting acquainted we arrived in Calcutta where we spent five nights in a Salvation Army bug-infested hostel for $2 a night. What a honeymoon!

Being the wife of Calvin called for a second surrender. To be a missionary is one thing, but to be a missionary wife is an entirely different calling. To give up independence at 31, surrender my career as nurse and teacher in a girls' boarding school, to change country and language, and as I found out later, to change lifestyle also, was not easy. As a woman, living in Muslim dominated East Pakistan was much more difficult than living in Hindu India.

With no real courtship and now no "honeymoon" we

left India to enter East Pakistan. We spent 7 hours at the border post for inspection by the custom officials. Since my last name had not yet been changed on my passport I pretended I was not married but rather my older brother, Calvin, was escorting me. This was easily understood in that culture. The word wedding would have caused a more detailed inspection of our luggage.

There were strict rules about purchasing items in India and taking them out of the country. On the station platform we observed piles of confiscated clothing, bedding, table covers etc., some similar to the wedding gifts packed in our gray trunk.

Officers were in and out of our compartment asking questions. One time they asked to see the gray trunk and discovered the wedding gown on top. I quickly explained it was a veil and they respected that privacy.

Calvin and I considered it prudent to not talk to each other. We even delayed eating our packed lunch for fear it would arouse suspicion. We had only been married six days.

At all the check posts, in airports, and in government offices, our Mission's name wasn't the easiest to explain. A.G. was often referred to as American God Mission. In India the title denotes more than one God: Assemblies of God of North India, and Assemblies of God of South India.

We spent the first two weeks in Khulna, a port city, with missionaries Orville and Yvonne Carlson and their three small children while waiting for my trunks to come by boat from India.

They lived in a house built on stilts, with wide cracks in the floor and walls made of bamboo matting. Rats ran around in the rafters at night and for breakfast we were served pancakes with large ants swimming in the syrup.

Like everyone else we just removed the ants and proceeded with the meal.

Leaving Hindu India where women had more liberties I was suddenly transported to the Muslim dominated culture of East Pakistan where women were seldom seen in public, always with an escort, and usually veiled. This called for some major adjustments.

The Lord let me know early in our marriage that Calvin had a special assignment. I was to understand that from now on he would fulfill God's will for both of us. Today I still consider Calvin a very special person. I was proud and privileged to be his wife, a missionary wife, for 44 years. His success became my legacy.

Chapter Eight

Pakistan
"A Holy Place for the Muslims"

Early on in our story, it is important to relate the formation and location of Pakistan. Since 1858 the British had ruled India. This rule ended in 1947 when Great Britain granted independence to India. The minority Muslim population insisted on having a segment of the land separate from Hindu India. Two areas where the majority population were Muslim became two provinces, East and West Pakistan, separated by 1700 miles of India. The name given to this new country, Pakistan, is translated as, "a holy land for the Muslim."

West Pakistan is 97 percent Muslim. It is bordered by Afghanistan on the west, North India on the east, and the Arabian sea on the south. A large portion of the country is desert. As compared to the people of East Pakistan, the people of West Pakistan are larger, with a fairer complexion, and eat bread and meat as a daily diet. A number of cultural groups live in various parts of this province. Each have their own distinctive characteristics and language such as Punjabi, Sindhi, Pushtu, Baluchi, and Urdu. The latter is of Arabic derivation and is considered the main language.

East Pakistan, (now Bangladesh) has a population that is 85 percent Muslim. This province was the underdeveloped delta portion of former India, east of Calcutta and bordering western Burma (now Myanmar). This hot, humid area of 55,598 square miles is home to 130 million people (as of year 2000) and its land mass is comparable to Iowa in the U.S., which has only three million people.

Much of Bangladesh is just above sea level with two large rivers, the Ganges and Jamuna, which originate in India. These rivers have many tributaries crisscrossing the country. Forty percent of the land area is flooded every year, posing an annual crisis.

The people are Asian, small in stature, with dark skin, black hair, and very dark eyes. Their diet consists of rice, fish, lentils, and vegetables. Their language is Bengali.

Fifty two percent of the population survive on one meal a day. Sixty percent are landless and thirty five percent are unemployed. Literacy is only thirty percent.

Here was a new country, consisting of two linguistically and culturally different provinces, separated by thousands of miles of unfriendly Indian territory. The common denominator was religion, but the language and culture were different. From the very beginning this was destined to be a tragedy. In 1971 a civil war erupted where West Pakistan invaded East Pakistan.

Chapter Nine

The Religion of Islam
"A Religion of Rules and Good Works"

I slam is a religion of rules and good works which has great control over its followers. The Muslim's allegiance to his religion, whereby he prays five times a day to Allah and questions nothing in his faith, is hard to penetrate. All are required to perform certain religious practices.

Because of the strong family unit, individual decisions are frowned upon. It is not uncommon for believers in Jesus as Savior, to hide their conversion for years, making public testimony rare. There are many secret believers in the Muslim world. Those who dare to reveal their new faith risk losing inheritance, imprisonment, or even death. They will most certainly be isolated from family, including wife and children.

When sharing with a Muslim we start with what we have in common in the Bible and Koran. The Koran contains parts of the Old testament and one of the Gospels. They believe in the virgin birth of Jesus. They believe He went to heaven without dying and will come again. They, however, reject Jesus as the Son of God.

Chapter Ten

A Woman's Role in Muslim Society
"Life Behind the Veil"

I would be spending many years in a Muslim country. As a woman, it was important that I understand the role of a female in that society. My remarks are a missionary's viewpoint, more specifically, a missionary to Bangladesh. You cannot live in a culture 35 years without being stamped by it. My life has been greatly influenced by what I have learned and has been enriched by the best of two cultures.

Islam is a way of life and a religion that veils many of their women. There are 485 million Muslim women in 50 countries of the world with different ethnic backgrounds. Educated or illiterate, rich or poor, married or single, homemakers or career women, many are veiled when they appear in public.

The veil is made of black, gray, or white coarse cotton or silk. The robe covers the woman from head to foot. Their world is seen through 2 x 4 inch patches of net covering the eyes. Most houses are built with an inner courtyard which completely separates the women from the public and limits her view of the outside.

The covering, worn only outside of the home, is to protect women from the gaze of men. The veil conceals her clothing and her jewelry (necklaces, bracelets, ear and nose rings), which are the family's bank account.

Not only is the veil uncomfortable in the heat but it is also potentially dangerous, as one's peripheral vision is limited. Some robes have no sleeves and no holes though which the arms can extend. Small children are carried under the robe and along with the mother, breathe air that is strained through the cloth of the veil-robe.

While touring the Islamic Society of North America in Plainfield, Indiana, we were surprised to discover that a daughter of a Methodist Minister, now a converted Muslim, was our guide. She was wearing a long tan colored dress, long sleeves, and a head covering that concealed hair and ears. When asked why she became a Muslim, she replied: "Islam liberated me as a woman. I no longer dress to please the opposite sex." At home, with her Muslim husband, she wore jeans and literally let her hair down.

Who wouldn't want to be free from sexual harassment, such as staring, winking, whistling, and pinching? If you wore the veil think of the money you would save from having to purchase name brand clothes, cosmetics, hair styling, or weight watcher's programs.

In one Muslim country a completely veiled woman remarked to a U.S. lady reporter, "Our veils conceal our tears." On the other hand a woman in an Asian country said she totally discarded the veil when her mother-in-law died. Others in that country have never worn the veil but follow certain rules of covering the head in public.

More important than the covering is the position of women in Islam. According to the Koran, Sura 4:34, the woman is inferior to man. She is a servant or slave, and men spend wealth (dowry) to obtain one. As his property she is subject to corporal punishment. Calvin made the mistake early in our career when he tried to stop a man who was beating his wife. The suffering wife turned to Calvin and told him to mind his own business. Good women are obedient. The man can beat her for disobedience and even isolate her for a period of time.

Women have a greater spiritual capacity than men though most of them cannot attend the mosque for public prayers. In their homes, however, many are faithful to unfold their little prayer rug, kneel facing Mecca, and pray five times a day.

I recall our hostess excusing herself and leaving the table before the meal was finished, to perform prayers at the set time. She had heard the "call to prayer" from the nearby mosque. The host remained with the guests. It had a sobering effect. The prayer rug, a religious symbol, is neatly rolled and placed in a special place for use at the next call to prayer.

The following rules were mine for 35 years as I endeavored to identify with the women and their culture. Women walk, don't run. In public they speak softly, do not raise their voice, and speak only to women. However, at home they are loudly heard.

They walk a few steps behind their husband and never address him in public. I would drop my eyes when a man would pass me on the path and even though he was a Christian and attended our church, I refrained from looking at him or speaking to him.

Women don't shake hands, but men may hold hands with other men when walking in public. I soon learned that women do not sit when any man is standing, including her husband. When guests visit, the women move to the bedroom where they sit cross legged on the bed while the men sit in another room.

In order to reach such women with the Gospel I had to earn the right to be heard by developing friendships. It helped for me to wear their national dress, learn their language and culture, learn how to cook their food, and as much as possible copy their traditions.

It was important for me to visit them in their home, or provide a "safe haven" where they could relax among women only. My home became such a haven where I developed many friendships, some of which continue to this day.

In witnessing to these new friends, I would first show interest in the woman as a person, rather than just her soul. At other times I just listened, answered questions, and served hot tea. I let them hear and see me pray, and recognize that I had a personal relationship with God. Later there were opportunities to share my spiritual experiences with them.

Chapter Eleven

Bengali–A Poetical Language
"Don't imagine by crossing the sea and landing on a foreign shore and learning a foreign language, you burst the bonds of outer sin and hatch yourself a cherubim."
–Amy Carmichael

M arriage brought many changes including a different language. I had studied and spoken the Hindi language in Bihar, North India. Now I must learn Bengali, the language of East Pakistan. The State Department of the United States lists Bengali as the most difficult language to learn.

We moved to the capital city, Dhaka, where for 18 months we continued language study with a private tutor. At that time there was no language school in the country and we were required to take the same final examination as those in India who had the privilege of a language school. This proved to be a challenge requiring much discipline. We studied eight hours daily, finishing the final exam in December 1956. It has been said that learning a language requires more incentive than aptitude.

We made many mistakes in learning the language. Some mistakes were laughable while others almost disastrous. Early in our career Calvin was preaching through an interpreter and used the following as an illustration. Calvin said, "We returned from a village tour and discovered the caretaker left in charge of our house was no where to be found. He had gone on a trip to visit relatives. When he returned it seemed necessary to fire him." The interpreter gave this translation. "Mr. Olson was so disappointed in the caretaker he shot him." Calvin knew just enough of the language to correct the mistake.

During one of Calvin's first attempts to preach in this new language he used the verse "Jesus said, I am the Light of the world." The word for light is "alo" and the word for potato is "alu." You guessed it. The whole sermon was "Jesus is the potato of the world." Gracious as they are no one laughed and no one corrected him until later. Since potatoes, however, are an important food source the message was not entirely lost on them. Jesus is provider as well.

Someone said the Bengali language is very expressive. I agree. Everyday I learned new phrases, idioms, and colloquialisms. One "Grandma" visited me often for more medicine for "the place where the baby comes out." Her son had insects eating his teeth (toothache).

Eventually we became comfortable with the Bengali language and found it a convenient second language abroad and even in the U.S.A. When we wanted to deliver a private message we would leave notes for each other written in Bengali.

Calvin could always get my attention in a crowd if he called out something in the Bengali language. Even now there are times when the Bengali word is on my tongue before the English word, and I must interpret for the listeners.

Since I had spent two years studying Hindi and had

attended a Bengali language school for three months prior to our marriage, I decided to forsake the books for one year. Perhaps as the wife of a missionary, it wasn't so important for me to do the second year exam. I could learn from listening. This helped me to adjust to marriage and to encourage Calvin in his study.

However two months before Calvin would take his final language exam he challenged me to try for the exam. These are his own words: "It is important for you to complete the second exam to set an example for younger missionaries."

Scanning his books, reading his notes, and drilling with him each day I accepted the challenge and passed the test. I must add that Hindi and Bengali grammar are quite similar though they do differ in script, spelling, and pronunciation. I have always been thankful for Calvin's encouragement, a quality he would continue to display throughout our marriage.

Chapter Twelve

Rest and Relief
"We remember we are but clay
that can easily crack and break."
–Marian N. Olson

After the stress of language study we were ready for a change in climate and work. We decided to visit the mountain area in North India where Calvin and I first met. The temperature would be cooler and the Mission's guest house, Childers Lodge, would provide complete relaxation. It would be a long two day journey by train via Calcutta.

The last two miles on our way up the mountains to Childers Lodge we would be carried in a chair (dandy) born on the shoulders of four men (dandy). Our reward would be the daily view of the sun shining on the snow covered Himalayan mountains in the distance, and the fresh clear air at nearly 7000 ft. above sea level.

Accommodations were simple but adequate. Mosquito nets were provided as the windows were unscreened. There was electricity but no running water. Water was stored in large clay pots in the bathroom. A movable basin was provided. Cup baths were the custom. One squats in a given area and from the clay pot large cups of water are poured over the body and the drippings flow out a hole in the wall.

For toilet facilities there was a wooden stool in the corner that had a lid that flopped up and down. Inside the stool was a removable pot which was emptied by a hired man once each day. This was somewhat of an improvement over an outhouse.

One experience during that holiday was unforgettable. The morning sun revealed hundreds of black specks on the outside top of our mosquito net. As we lay there trying to identify the spots they began to move and we realized we were surrounded by bed bugs. Trying not to disturb them we exited the net, quickly dressed, and made our escape. Fumigation took care of the plague temporarily but we did not sleep there again. Whitewashing the walls had not destroyed the bug population. We, however, could not brag about even one bite.

It was early summer and we spent most of the days outside enjoying the variety of flowers and mountain air. I had just learned that I was pregnant with our first child. One day I discovered an unusual skin rash which proved to be German measles. I learned later there was an epidemic among the children in the boarding school nearby.

The doctor examining me mentioned that since I was pregnant there was a chance of aborting the unborn baby. If there was a normal delivery, statistics revealed the baby would be affected in some way by exposure to measles. Looking back on those long eight months I rather enjoyed my pregnancy denying anything abnormal, and believing all would go well.

One Sunday morning, after returning to Dhaka, Calvin and I were badly jolted when the three wheel rickshaw we were riding in hit a hole in the road. I was eight months pregnant. Immediately I felt abdominal pain so we headed for the local hospital.

After a brief examination the doctor announced that our baby had stopped breathing. With limited facilities and outdated equipment I was left to wait out the five days of labor. Calvin could only visit me certain hours. As our still born daughter made her appearance I lost consciousness.

Baby "Jan," whom I never saw, was handed to Calvin wrapped in a newspaper. According to the law burial must take place before dark the same day. Dressing the baby for burial, hiring a carpenter to make a small box, Calvin proceeded to the cemetery four miles away.

We had no vehicle other than a bicycle, and no public conveyance would take a corpse. An American, serving with a U.S. aid program, heard of our plight and offered his car. Calvin placed the tiny box in the freshly dug hole and recited the committal ceremony.

This was my first and last pregnancy. Sometime later, I discovered this poem which described my feelings for years to come.

> *I used to love this sunny room with shiny*
> *windows in a row;*
> *It overlooks my neighbor's yard, and here I'd*
> *sit to write or sew.*
> *Since a certain day last spring a pain burns*
> *at my heart's core.*
> *Though I protest I don't know why I never*
> *sit there any more.*
> *Nor write my foolish rhymes; yet deep within*

this aching soul of mine,
I know it is the baby clothes which flutter on
my neighbor's line.
                                    –By Martha Snell Nicholson

Beginnings

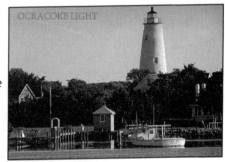

Marian's birthplace

Marian's family picture (Marian is second from the right)

Marian on board English freighter departing for India, 1950

Marian studying Hindi
language with private
tutor in India

Marian with Indian
women traveling
to a village

Baby born in a
stable

Calvin's family (Calvin on far right)

Calvin (right) holding Bible at early age

Calvin with Orville Carlson on hunting trip to jungle, Bangladesh, 1955

Calvin and Marian traveling by rickshaw

Calvin and Marian
meet in India, 1954

Calvin and
Marian married
in India, 1955

PART TWO
Gopalganj and Village Life

"Lord, Give me the strength lightly to bear my joys and sorrows.

give me the strength to make my love fruitful in service.

give me the strength never to disown the poor.

Give me the strength to raise my mind high above daily trifles.

Give me the strength to surrender my strength to Thy will with love."

–Poet, Rabindraneth Tagore
(Translated from the Bengali Language)

Chapter Thirteen

Gopalganj
"The Joy of Simplicity"

Some of the names given to Bangladesh by visitors are: "The Basket Case of the World" and "Land of Heaped-up Heart Ache." It was in this Muslim country, one of the poorest in the world, that my husband Calvin and I made a life long commitment to serve. We began our service in the small town of Gopalganj.

Bangladesh is one of the more populous nations of Southern Asia with over 130 million people. It is the fourth largest Islamic nation in the world. It is one of the few Islamic nations that has a secular government which on paper assures religious freedom to all.

They export more jute than any country in the world, grow tea and rice, and manufacture their own paper products. Due to over population they depend upon imports of rice, the staple food. In recent years their clothing factories have provided exports to many countries of the world and are known for their excellent craftsmanship.

The country has suffered so much in its struggle for independence. About one million people perished during the war for liberation from the Western Province. Additionally, frequent natural disasters batter this nation, bringing destruction and untold suffering on these beautiful people. In 1970 half a million people died in a tidal wave during a severe cyclone. The people of this small densely populated country are among the most resilient in the world. It is amazing how though they lose everything many times they can begin again with nothing.

Our first assignment was to plant a church in Gopalganj, a subdivisional town only accessible by boat. Gopalganj is an eight hour boat ride from the port city, Khulna. Calvin lived in a one room, mud floor, grass roof house while supervising the construction of our future home. After the loss of our baby, I remained for a time in the capital city of Dhaka to regain my strength.

One night during construction, while sleeping in the hut, Calvin was awakened several times by a dull rhythmic thud. Each time after checking with his flashlight he returned to his folding cot only to be awakened again. In the morning he discovered a man-size hole dug through the mud foundation of his hut. Someone must have known he had money to pay laborers the next day. Calvin's deliverance was the first of many miracles we were to experience. That same night thieves stole a boat in the nearby canal.

Leaving a comparatively modern furnished apartment in Dhaka I eventually joined Calvin to make our first home in the primitive village setting, a three room brick building with cement floors and a tin roof. There was no electricity or plumbing. Water was carried from the village well. Cooking was done on a kerosene stove and oil lamps provided light. The plastered inside walls were white washed; the wooden table, chairs, and window frames remained unpainted; and the gray cement floors without carpets.

Calvin made a clothes closet out of the crate that the outboard motor was shipped in. Metal drums (barrels) were used for protecting clothes from moths and rats. Bedspreads were not necessary. I cut up bed sheets and fitted them onto bamboo poles to serve as curtains. Our one luxury was a western type toilet which was flushed with a pail of water. From 1956-1962 this was to be our home. Amazingly, I was happy!

Some estimates say that three out of five people in Bangladesh are without employment. However, as in many third world countries, they have learned to exist on very little. Most families in this country live on about $15 a month. This is how: Boys marry and live with their parents on their family land where they can grow bamboo, khus grass, and jute for house building and repairs. Trees provide firewood for winter fires, and cooking. A small plot of land supplies grain, fruit, and vegetables which allows them to raise a goat or cow. Selling produce and milk, they use the money to buy things they can't grow, such as cooking oil, soap and clothes.

Their water comes from the village well, river, or canal. They live by sun time, rise and retire early with no need for watches. They use only hand operated tools for plowing, cutting, threshing, and winnowing rice and wheat. Sand and ashes are used for washing cooking pots. Cow dung mixed with water serves as polish for the mud floor A twig plucked daily from the neem tree makes a great tooth brush by first chewing one end till it becomes like bristles.

Fuel for cooking is dried leaves, branches, dried cow dung, and stalks from jute and rice plants. Cooking is done in brass, aluminum or clay pots over a hole in the ground and food is eaten with one's fingers. Clothing is simple and minimal. They go barefoot or make their own sandals from straw and rope. Hand sewn children's clothes are made from recycled adult clothing and quilts are made from several layers of worn out saris (5 1/2 yards of material). Clothes are laundered in the nearest stream, river, or canal. Salt is used for medicine and preservation of food.

With limited cash flow the school teacher is paid with a meal a week or rice from one's field. Children's school books are often hand copied. At midday, enough food is cooked for two feedings and is not reheated for the second meal. This conserves fuel. People buy nothing that they can live without and every member of the family has assigned responsibilities. If one does not own land then life becomes even more difficult.

The poetical language of this eastern province, Bengali, is a derivative of Sanskrit, as are many Indian languages. It is spoken by more people than French as a mother tongue. The people are gifted in drama, poetry, and are talented musicians. Two unique instruments are the sitar, a stringed instrument, and the harmonium. The latter is a miniature organ with piano keyboard played with the right hand and bellows played with the left. The well known nobel prize-winning poet, Rabindranath Tagore, was a Bengali.

Chapter Fourteen

The Village House
"House has windows, door, and roof;
Home is where you are together!
–Marian N. Olson

From our centrally located town Calvin would take two week tours of churches in the district to encourage pastors and to promote evangelism. I would remain at home, the only white face in the community and the only one who spoke English. The moment I left my house I stepped into another culture with female veiled forms moving in a line on a narrow path with only feet and hands showing. I would not recognize my neighbor if I passed her in public.

Out of curiosity some women came to visit me. We sat on mats on the grass. Wondering what I wear under my long dress, the women lifted my skirt to examine the slip and whatever. It was then I felt the need of dressing like them. From behind this made me look like one of them and I found it easier to move about and visit the ladies in their homes.

A typical village home is a one room dwelling with sun-baked mud floor, thatched roof, and walls made of woven bamboo matting or mud. The family bed occupies most of the floor space and serves by day as a sitting and dining area where they comfortably sit with legs crossed. A chair is considered a status symbol. Often this rare piece of furniture would be loaned from house to house for a foreign visitor. The whole family sleeps on a large bed and even visitors share it at night, as we often did.

When it rains and the outdoor stove cannot be used, the wife cooks on a portable mud stove placed on the bed. There is usually one small window and a low doorway. The door is closed only at night and secured often with a thick wooden bar for protection from intruders. Sandals, if they own them, are left out side to protect the mud floor which is kept polished with a mixture of fresh cow dung and water. Amazingly the floor shines after such treatment.

A metal trunk with a lock, containing best clothes and other valuables, is stored under the bed along with cooking utensils, a homemade broom, clay pots of rice, and lentils. For protection, the goat and chickens may sleep under the bed at night. I recall sleeping on a bed of split bamboos in a lean-to porch with goats, their kids and chickens. Throughout the night the kids would bleat for their mother and she would reply. At day break, the rooster would announce it was time to wake up. Fortunately village people are sound sleepers. I wasn't.

There may be a separate shed that they use as a kitchen. Here one can cook year round and visit with neighbors. Fuel is anything that will burn. Often cow dung is pressed around short branches and left to dry in the sun before becoming fuel. A common sight is a pile of straw held together by a center bamboo pole, situated near the cooking area. One reaches for a handful of straw with the left hand to feed the fire while the right hand stirs the rice in the kettle. Often I would fuel the fire with straw or dung cakes while my neighbor cooked. With only one burner the food cooked first is cold by the time the meal is ready. I noticed they never apologized for serving cold food, so that is acceptable.

Rice is the main food eaten at least twice a day with green vegetables, fish or lentils. Left over rice is stored in water overnight in all kinds of temperatures, and eaten the next morning with fresh hot green peppers. Everyone can have free fish if they catch it. The country is crisscrossed with rivers, canals, and streams. Usually there is a man-made pond within walking distance. All contain fish and one does not need a license to fish. Grandmothers are often delegated to sit on the bank for hours to catch the daily protein. They will eat any green plant that is not poisonous. I have had neighbors ask if they could pick the weeds in my yard. Also their cows and goats kept my lawn trimmed so there was no need for a lawn mower.

One morning when Calvin and I were guests in a village home we had our first meal at 10 a.m. It consisted of cold rice left over from the night before, with some spicy fish caught in the pond. For hours during the day we visited and talked with people. In the evening Calvin taught in the village church for a couple hours. We were exhausted and hungry, and we avoided carrying snacks lest we insult our host. We, however, did have such treats for our long day trips by boat. Since there was no sign of food preparation we decided to go to sleep on a platform of split bamboos located on a lean-to porch.

When daylight fades there is no electricity so one must depend upon a flashlight or kerosene lamp. Not only to escape the darkness, but also to escape the mosquitoes we chose to go to bed early. Sleep that seemed so inviting earlier, was now sheer torture as our bed of uneven bamboo slats poked us in the back. Since the mosquito net was our only privacy I retired fully clothed in 95 percent humidity.

At 2 a.m. we were awakened by our host announcing that it was meal time. We were served cold turtle curry cooked in mustard oil. We learned that the biweekly market was two miles away and further delays were due to social visits at the market making the meal later than usual. Most people don't have watches and at night the sun does not tell time.

Most people in Bangladesh eat their second meal of the day around 10 p.m., which is an ideal time with the cows in the stall, and darkness shielding them from the sun. Usually the men and children eat first and, often from the same large brass plate. When they have been adequately served the wife, sometimes seated beside the smoking embers of the dying fire, would eat whatever food is left.

During one of our tours, Calvin and that village's pastor went to a neighboring village while the pastor's wife and I worked for two hours preparing a meal. Whey they returned around 10 p.m. we served them rice, fish, lentils and vegetables. As long as they asked for more their plates were refilled which resulted in my hostess and I sitting in the cook shed, eating rice and salt. This was not uncommon.

On another occasion I waited with my hostess for our two men to return from a visit to a distant village. It was midnight. We decided to make pancakes (pita) from rice flour. Later these would be dipped in date palm syrup as a treat for them. I sat on a low stool before the fire keeping it alive with dung cakes and straw which I pulled from a nearby haystack. Dew was falling which cooled the earth and our damp bodies. The stars and finally the moon made their appearance and I must say the whole scene suggested romance. By the time the men arrived, however, the rice pancakes were cold and we were tortured by mosquitoes.

Chapter Fifteen

Village Culture
*"What a man does is less important
than what he is."*
–A. W. Tozer

While visiting one village home I noticed a three legged unpainted chair leaning against the mud wall of the house. It had been borrowed for me, the Westerner, who perhaps was not accustomed to sitting on the ground. When we were served our meal I noticed there were two glasses. Often we only found one glass in a home. One had been borrowed from the neighbors. There were times I knew they could not afford the "feast" they had prepared for us. The large clay pot for storing rice was empty and the fuel pile was exhausted. Within two hours, unbelievably, a meal was set before us. They taught me hospitality with sacrifice.

I was soon introduced to some strange new customs. Men wear skirts for casual wear while women in the village wear only a sari (5 1/2 yards of material draped around the body, minus a blouse and petticoat). I've watched the men clean their nose with their finger and wipe it on a tree trunk or on their clothes while the women would use part of their clothing for the same purpose. Westerners, however, clean their nose with a square piece of cloth and store it in their pocket for future use. As for a tooth brush, a finger dipped in charcoal does a fine job.

Having a good sense of smell was not a plus. My nose was attacked by many new and different odors. There were open latrines, piles of garbage in the neighborhood and the smell of rotten meat and fish in the open markets. A favorite cooking oil was processed from mustard seeds and used for frying fish or used as a substitute for salad dressing. It was also used for rubbing on the body to keep the skin moist or as a remedy for sore muscles. This tangy oil penetrated clothes, hair, food and bedding. At first these new customs were quite offensive but soon, we also were sleeping with the family, sitting on the floor, eating the same food and even rubbing mustard oil on our bodies.

What we consider private is not observed as privacy in the culture of the village. We soon learned that "What is yours is mine." One borrows without returning. You can ask personal questions. You can read any mail lying around. People enter without knocking after giving a series of coughs as they approach a house. A stranger might walk up to two people talking privately and enter into the conversation. Bribing and lying is an acceptable way of life. A person may visit you for an hour and then just before leaving tell you why he came.

Children are given names with specific meanings like: star, moon, sun and a variety of flowers. Birds are given descriptive names like the Suti-Churi bird which when translated means "needle thief." The legend goes like this, "A lady in the moon was sewing and a bird stole her needle and attached it to his tail." The bird's tail actually looks like a long needle.

Chapter Sixteen

The Postman Doesn't Knock
"Service is love in working clothes."
–Unknown

How very important and difficult are the postal services for the village people in Bangladesh, a country crisscrossed by rivers big and small. Millions of letters and post cards are annually delivered by foot, some to people with no fixed address. Since 85 percent of the people live in villages, the mail carrier must walk, balancing two heavy mailbags, one on either end of a pole supported by his shoulder. In one hand he carries a pole from the top end of which is attached bells constantly ringing to announce his arrival. In the other hand he carries a kerosene lantern because quite frequently his trip continues long after it is dark as he journeys to out of the way places.

His memory of the faces has to be unique and his deductive reasoning has to be superb so that he can locate his addressee who may be a hawker sitting in one corner of the area's daily open market. Tomorrow the same hawker may be sitting in another area.

The foot postman must be very strong, have uncanny horse sense, and a great amount of courage. He also needs dexterity for negotiating "bridges" which actually may be just a plank or one bamboo pole thrown across a canal or small river. The foot postman is vital to the postal system which would simply collapse without him. He carries the mail to and from distant villages which do not have any direct link with the nearest towns.

The postman with extraordinary memory for faces and names reaches out to distant rural areas and delivers the letters and money orders which may come from distant places like the U.K. or U.S.A. by airmail. The village folk not only do not have their houses numbered but more often than not get letters inadequately, indistinctly and even wrongly addressed.

Such mail would have remained undelivered at the post offices of the town up to which the mail packets reached were it not for these foot postmen. Instead of the familiar post office known to us, outgoing mail may be deposited at a designated shop in the market place and later collected by the postman. In spite of the fact that these "deliverers of mail" are poorly paid they are highly responsible and resourceful to ensure, at least in most cases, the proper delivery of money orders and letters.

Chapter Seventeen

The Dying and Dead
*"I wondered why somebody didn't do something,
then I realized I was somebody."*
—Unknown

It has been said that if a child in Bangladesh survives to the age of five he has a chance to live to become an adult. When we went to this country in 1954 the average life span was 47 years. In 1990 it was 52. One day a 40 year old woman told me she was old and was going to die soon. She looked like death. I was old enough to be her mother but she looked older than I. Many die young due to the lack of proper medical aid or misuse of drugs sold without prescription or lack of finances to see a doctor.

With no special home for the mentally ill, families are left to deal with situations on their own. One day as we were walking through a neighborhood we noticed a naked man chained to the trunk of a tree. We heard later that often he would break loose and wander through the village. One day while shopping for food in an open market area, a scantily clad man began to follow us repeating phrases in his language which we understood. We knew he was mad and his slogans were directed toward us. We needed to escape somehow. A crowd was following him, laughing and rather enjoying the performance. Turning, we noticed he was lighting matches and putting them in his mouth. This of course was highly entertaining to the crowd. The thought utmost in our minds, however, was, "This man needs deliverance. What would Jesus do?"

Calvin was most embarrassed one day as he was driving alone in an open jeep down the streets of Khulna, one of the port cities. He had to travel slowly to avoid hitting cows, goats, chickens, and people. Suddenly someone jumped up on the hood of the jeep. To his amazement it was a naked woman with matted hair and covered with dried mud. Not knowing what move to make Calvin just sat behind the wheel ready to drive on whenever she would move. A crowd soon gathered and people began to laugh at her, at the situation, and at Calvin. The minutes seemed like hours before someone coaxed her down and led her away. Life is raw in many ways in such an impoverished society.

Since we did not lock our doors during the day people would sometimes walk in without knocking. On this particular day I walked from the bedroom to the room that served as cooking, eating, and sitting area. A mentally ill man wearing only a loin cloth was eating a banana he had taken from the fruit bowl on the table. Not knowing how to handle the situation and also since I was a woman, I quickly exited the back door and called for Calvin. Letting the man know he was lost and had come to the wrong house Calvin led him outside, down the path and handed him over to neighbors. Many have fallen into the fire, into the pond, canal or river, and even wandered away from home for weeks at a time. This of course is cause of great concern to family members and frustrating to all concerned.

I shall never forget the first Christian funeral I attended. Badal, a prematurely old man about 40 years of age died at noon. Since there is no provision for embalming one must be buried before sunset. Badal's friends and relatives hurried to hire a carpenter to make a six sided box, larger at the head than the foot. Muslims, however, do not use a box but only a shroud. The corpse is carried by four men on a board or rope bed from the house to the cemetery, no matter how great the distance. Due to superstition no public conveyance can be hired.

With the sound of hammer and nails nearby this Christian wife prostrated herself on her husband's motionless body and began to wail, caressing his body, talking to him and begging his forgiveness. The corpse was then laid on a mat on the ground where it was washed in full view of neighbors and friends. Some insist on certain kinds of soap and then mustard oil for rubbing on the body and coconut oil for the head. The wife insisted on bathing him as no one else knew how he liked his bath. Since this was not acceptable I helped to restrain her trembling body while the bathing proceeded.

After the body was draped in a sheet with only the face showing it was laid in the finished box and carried to the church. They knew we owned a camera so they requested a photo. Everyone present wanted to be in the picture no matter how they were dressed, including the mud covered bodies of the young boys who were hired to dig the grave. The grave diggers soon struck water and someone else had to bail out the water. The digging and bailing went on for some time and then a sudden rain shower caused further delay. The boys covered with mud ran around in the rain for their daily shower. The body was finally laid to rest at twilight. Often a hired group will wail during the whole procedure but for the Christians who believe in the resurrection, the sting of death is less painful.

I have often been called upon to bathe a woman or child and assist the family in securing a box. Each time I am reminded of our only child buried among other Christians in a cemetery in the capital city of Dhaka, awaiting the resurrection.

Chapter Eighteen

Village Churches
"Churches have walls. People have hearts."
–Marian N. Olson

Village churches have sunbaked mud floors and walls of mud or woven bamboo matting with a grass roof. A more prosperous church would have brick walls, cement floors, and a tin roof. The windows are always open. There are cracks in the walls and lots of room for spiders, lizards, mosquitoes, and mice.

Unlike city churches there are no chairs in village churches. Mats are spread on the floor with a narrow isle dividing men from women. Women are expected to sit on one side with the children and men on the other side. It is not unusual for the children to run back and forth between mom and dad. When I first saw this in church I thought it rather irreverent and undisciplined but it did not seem to disturb anyone.

Women cover their heads with a portion of their sari in church. Unless this is secured to the hair it keeps falling down revealing their long black hair. It is interesting to watch the hands move up and down replacing the covering each time it falls.

The Bible is treated with much respect, usually handled with both hands. It is never placed on the floor except when one is seated on the floor and then in such a position that it is not touched by the feet. It is common to cover the Bible with a cloth to protect it from dust.

When Holy Communion is observed and traditional grape juice is not available, pink, highly scented rose water is served in a common cup. One out of ten people in the country have tuberculosis. Along with others I have drunk from such a cup without contacting the disease.

Shoes are for outside wear only. They are removed before entering a home or church. It is amusing and amazing to see a hundred people looking for their shoes at the end of the church service, a task made even more difficult by the children who played with them during the service. Seldom are shoes stolen, but believe it or not, a missionary's size twelve shoes disappeared during one church service. No one in that country would have feet that large.

Since most babies are naked from the waist down, often the mothers miss the cue to take them outside and little puddles form on the church floor which the mother quickly wipes with "whatever" is available. When this happens on the cement floor next to the piano pedal in our city church, a newspaper, kept handy for such emergencies, serves well.

I am reminded of an incident during a song service in a village church. A mouse suddenly appeared and seemed uninhibited, fearless and even tame as it ran among the congregation who were sitting barefoot on mats on the floor. Finally a man grabbed it and stuck it under his garments. When the preacher started to speak he released the mouse which began to play and disturb the meeting. The preacher stopped and waited until it was caught again and taken outside where it was released, not killed. The meeting proceeded.

Weddings

The practice of "dowry" for a bride still exists. The groom-to-be could demand anything. A poor girl therefore had to settle for a poor man who was often uneducated as well. I recall attending a Christian wedding in the village, with just five minutes notice. A family member personally invites each guest and in some cases hands them a printed invitation. It would be rude and expensive to mail the invitation or send it by a non-family member. Our "invite" came late.

When I arrived at the church the bride, heavily veiled, was sitting on the front bench waiting for the groom to arrive. Beside her was a boy about 7 years of age, no doubt a relative, completely naked. The mother of the bride spit out the open window during the ceremony. The preacher's son enjoyed climbing in and out of the window while his father was preaching. The bride refused to speak and repeat the vows. Several from the audience scolded her with shouts of, "speak up." She was 15 years old while the man was 40 plus.

Since it was expensive to marry off girls, parents would often give one of their many daughters, between seven and eleven years of age, to work in a stranger's home. She may be an orphan or one of many sisters who was a liability to parents. Forfeiting education and comforts she served as water carrier, dishwasher, baby-sitter and housekeeper in exchange for meals and shelter. Some even became so attached to the family they blended in with their children.

Chapter Nineteen

The Big Day
"Christmas in Bangladesh"

December 25, "Boro Din" (The big Day), is better known as Christmas in the West. Since Christians are a very small minority in this Muslim country Christmas is celebrated in a very different way. There is nothing in the stores or on the streets to remind one of this special holiday. However, the government recognizes it as a special holiday for Christians only and most employers excuse Christians from their jobs on that day.

A week in advance a planned drama will be performed under a tent in the parking lot for community entertainment. In more recent years, in the capital city, the church choir presents a concert, "The Singing Christmas Tree." The tree frame is made of long bamboos tied together with jute rope and covered with bright green cloth. Wooden planks are then arranged to accommodate the choir. The finished structure, with colored lights, built on the church parking lot, would end up being as high as a two story building. With open sky and palm trees in the background it attracts hundreds. Many who cannot find sitting space are willing to stand for the hour's performance. Up to 2,000 people of all religions witness this portrayal of the birth of Jesus with the choir singing in three languages; Bengali, English, and Swedish.

The celebration of Christmas Day is very much church oriented. Instead of decorating their homes days in advance, the members drape the church walls and ceiling fans (in the city) with colorful handmade decorations from crepe paper. Since the decorations are so elaborate and much time is spent creating them, they remain up sometimes for three months or until they fall down.

The whole night before Christmas Day, groups travel to Christian homes, singing the familiar carols and being rewarded with candy or hot tea and cookies. All night, volunteers help prepare a feast for the following day. Over several holes in the ground, platforms of bricks are built to support large kettles which are rented for the occasion. Wood and dry leaves are used for fuel. Onions, garlic, ginger root and spices are ground between two stones. One stone is large and rectangular in shape while the smaller one is shaped like an American rolling pin. Early on the morning of the 25th, the live chickens, imprisoned under coarsely woven baskets are brought to the parking lot for execution. Each one does it's headless death dance as it flops around in the dust before being skinned.

Christians start to gather at the church around 8:30 a.m. wrapped in shawls and wearing sweaters as it is winter (50 degrees by night and up to 75 by day). Hot tea and dried toast (similar to American rusks) are served to each one before the special Christmas service in the church. At 1 p.m. the food is ready to be served. This is a typical Bengali meal of rice and spicy vegetables and meat, with better than daily fare. All sit cross legged, knee to knee, on woven mats or burlap spread on the cement or mud floor .

Each person is given a plate, if available, or banana leaf, and a glass of water. In some places they must bring their own glass. With the left hand they pour water over the right hand, dripping it over their plate. Then with the right hand wash the plate. Someone comes around with a pail to collect the water from the plates. With clean hands and washed plate they are ready to eat.

A barefoot man with the use of a saucer or half coconut shell ladles a generous portion of rice from a woven basket onto each plate. Women do not serve in public but are very much a servant in the home. This, however, is a special day for the women. The women not only get to eat at the same time as the men and children but they also are served by men. Another man serves fried spicy fish or eggplant. When everyone is served, the chatter stops and the pastor leads in prayer. They do not pray over empty plates. When the first course is finished they are served spicy chicken and potatoes in a gravy and salad. Eating with fingers of the right hand only, caution is taken not to let the food touch the palm of the hand. The desert may be either sweetened yogurt or rice pudding.

When a person is finished eating he rinses his right hand over the empty plate using water from his glass. In a few minutes the hand is dry, no need for a towel. They may take the glass of water to a nearby flower bed or tree and rinse their hands so the water can fall on the ground. The floor becomes messy as during the meal any part which they prefer not to eat (bones, whole spices etc.) is removed from the plate. A volunteer clean-up crew removes the plates and sweeps the floor or ground. Then the cooking and serving crews sit and eat together. Anywhere from 50 to 500 share the celebration in groups throughout the country.

People remain for another hour or more visiting with family and friends in the sun. They are reluctant to leave the church and garden and return to their congested living quarters. The evenings are spent visiting from house to house drinking tea and eating traditional fruitcake, purchased at the many bakeries who prepare it just for this Christian holiday. Drinking tea in each other's homes is like breaking the bread of fellowship, no matter how humble the dwelling.

It was after visiting the last home for tea and cake that Calvin and I prepared to leave. It was dusk and we had neglected to bring a flashlight, expecting to return home before dark. Noticing we were leaving without a light, our neighbor offered to lend us a lantern. The path was narrow. Calvin was walking ahead swinging the smoking lantern forward and backward to give us both maximum light when suddenly he stopped and yelled "samp." Walking closely behind I bumped into him before I could stop. We waited until the snake disappeared into the bushes and then proceeded home. That neighbor's lantern could have saved our lives.

Chapter Twenty

Convention – Village Style
"They set up a tabernacle in the wilderness."

Annual Christian conventions are often convened in a village setting where there is more space and better accommodations. One such gathering will forever remain in my memory. Calvin and I were to set up camp for missionaries and national pastors in a remote village which meant arriving at least one day in advance. It was a fourteen hour trip to the convention site by "noka," a small boat that traveled two miles an hour. Often Calvin and I would walk on the uneven sun baked mud bank of the canal so the boat could move faster.

Near the end of the journey a sudden northwest storm with strong winds and pelting rain began tossing our little boat around in the water of the canal. By now it was dark and we could see very little by the kerosene lantern. The wind increased to 75 mph. The boatman frantically tried to use his oar to balance the boat. When the oar was swept out of reach he used his body as a rudder to keep the boat from capsizing. Calvin and I were sitting under the curved roof of the boat, locked in by our luggage which was stored at both ends. The canal was not deep nor wide but in such a position we could not move. Prayer was our only hope.

Just as quickly as it came the storm passed and all was quiet again. Retrieving his oar the boatman continued our journey. Upon arrival that night, tired and wet, we learned that the convention had been postponed. Communication once again had failed. After a night in the village we returned home.

After two weeks we made the journey once again. There were three missionary couples, three children and three single ladies to plan for. It meant taking cooking utensils, breakfast and snack food, and a supply of drinking water until we could get a fire going and boil drinking water for our party. The last two miles of the journey was on foot as the canal water was not deep enough for the boat. This meant hiring men to carry all our luggage. I watched as the men sorted and loaded each other, on heads, backs, and arms. One picked up a large clay jug of water and decided it would be easier to carry it empty so proceeded to pour our precious supply of drinking water onto the muddy path. It was too late to protest and they wouldn't understand if we did. They survived without boiling their drinking water. Why shouldn't we?

The last lap of the journey was by foot over a very narrow path which served as a boundary between two rice fields. It was the rainy season so we found ourselves walking in mud. I was having balance problems. Calvin advised me to take short quick steps so my feet would not have time to sink into the mud. Then it happened. I stepped on a submerged piece of slippery bamboo and fell face forward in the mud. We both laughed as Calvin captured it on film. I was glad I was wearing the national dress, sari, so it was easy to exchange for a clean one behind our big black umbrella, right out in open country.

Later on we came to a break in the elevated path which allowed water to flow from one field to another. I could not jump the distance or wade so Calvin decided to carry me. When we both began to sink into the mud we had to be rescued by farmers working in the fields nearby. There was no one to take our picture this time. I wondered how the men described that to their wife and children.

Before the rest of the party would arrive there must be a toilet arrangement. Calvin cleared a path through the jungle to a conveniently secluded place and proceeded to dig a hole in the ground. Burlap sacking was stretched around four bamboo poles which had staked out the "hole" with an entrance facing the interior of the jungle. Nearby he made a similar roofless tent for a bath house. One of the committee members walked six miles to the nearest market to purchase supplies for the convention. Wood was cut and neatly piled near a hole which would serve as a stove. A large kettle produced from our luggage was filled with water from a tube well and set on the crude stove to boil for safe drinking water. Guarding it was my responsibility.

One family in the village loaned us their one room house for the four days. A bed sheet was hung to separate the ladies and children from the three missionary men. We slept in our bed rolls in a row like crayons in a box. The lack of privacy was something I would always struggle with. If one did not rise before daylight you could be sure eyes would be peeking through the woven bamboo walls or someone would wander into your area looking for a stray chicken or goat or to retrieve some cooking pan. We slept in the clothes we had worn all day so I was fully dressed when I crawled out of the bed roll. The wrinkled, faded look was always in vogue. That night rats had visited us and chewed on two Tupperware plastic lids rendering them useless.

Lunch and supper would be eaten with the rest of the 300 or more campers, but our small group would have a western breakfast of oatmeal, toast, bananas, and tea. It was my duty to make the tea. Squatting before the stove, I endeavored to pour hot water into the cups which were arranged on the ground. My position shifted and so did the tea kettle. The boiling water sprayed my left foot, leaving me incapacitated for the rest of the convention. Nature, however, has a way of healing, if given time.

Bathing during a convention while hundreds of people are milling around was something else. We tried to erect bath houses with five foot high bamboo matting supported by bamboo poles with a flimsy burlap door. There were two, one for women and one for men. Each person carried his own pail of water from the village pump or river and with an empty tin can dipped the water over his body after a good soaping. Taller bathers were easily identified but no one could enjoy privacy because of the peep holes. Again we bathed fully clothed.

You could choose to bathe in the canal, and most did; especially the men and children. The first time I tried to bathe in a river or pond without a washcloth or towel, and wearing all my clothes, ended in a fiasco. Concentrating on not stirring up the mud from the bottom, I gingerly stepped into the cloudy water. I knew this same water served for washing clothes, pots and pans, and bathing the cows. Using loose clothing as a washcloth I rubbed my body with soap. Dipping into the water several times I rinsed well and then climbed the muddy bank to dry land. Alas, the muddy water was now muddier as I had brought the mud bottom to the top. No one else could bathe until the mud settled to the bottom. This type of bathing is an art which must be learned. I never learned. I much preferred the "pail and cup" bath.

Exchanging wet clothes for dry ones without revealing white skin was a juggling act. The clean dry clothes quickly absorbed the moisture on your body leaving you still wet but with a clean feeling. What a treat to be able to bathe in the clear unrecycled water of a sudden shower of rain. I have memories of children dancing with glee in the refreshing water from above. I never complained when in our travels I had to walk miles in the rain. Bathing usually took place just before eating the noon meal. One's body is relaxed and food seemed to taste better.

Washing clothes was coupled with bathing your body. As soon as you exchanged the wet clothes for the dry, everyone, even the men, were expected to wash their own clothes in the same water. These might be spread to dry on bushes nearby, on tree branches, or on a makeshift line of two twisted strands of jute rope. The clothes would be held on the line by pressing the ends through the twist in the rope, a great substitute for clothes pins. During the dry season when dust was plentiful it would stick to the wet clothes leaving a gray look and dusty scent.

During conventions, three meetings each day were held under a large tent in the center of the village. For several years, we used unbleached dish towels sent by women in America, to make the tent. These were sewed together and proved quite durable in the sun and rain. Burlap bags, bamboo woven mats, carpeting, and even old bedding was used to spread on the ground for the people to sit on.

The people filled every available space as they folded their legs and sat knee to knee. Fellowship means "touching skin" and conventions allow for great fellowship. Up to 2,000 would attend the evening services which were open to all. Services were long, too long for the children who ran in and out of the meeting looking for parents. Our white skin, especially that of missionary children, is a distraction. On one occasion when a missionary mother took her blonde haired daughter out of the meeting, a long procession of dark skinned and black haired children followed.

Chapter Twenty-One

Storms, Floods, and Riots
"Whom the gods would destroy
they first make mad."
–Greek Origin

T he Bay of Bengal is bordered by India on the west, and Myanmar (Burma) on the east, with 357 miles of jagged coastline of Bangladesh on the north. Cyclones, birthed in the Bay threaten the lowlands every year. Tidal waves, which often form in these great storms travel inland as far as 30 miles, often causing severe devastation. Wind and rain storms from the northwest are common at certain times of the year. These freak storms usually come suddenly in the afternoons and pass just as quickly. The strong winds and rain can cause much damage to trees and buildings. Annual floods are the result of monsoon rains from May to October.

One night we were wakened by the sound of the rain battering the tin roof of our three room house. It had been raining for hours and now the wind had increased. From the window we could see the palm trees bend over to the ground and spring back while some had already submitted to the storm. We knew this could be a bad one so we did not try to sleep. Then we heard screaming which grew louder and came closer. People were rushing toward our house. Due to the strong winds we could hardly open the door to let them in. By then the thatched-roof, mud-floor houses all around us had collapsed and we had 50 rain drenched people, including babies crammed into two rooms. Thankful for a dry safe place they sat on mats on the floor to wait out the storm.

Rain continued all night and the next day. We exhausted our supply of rice and lentils for the enlarged family. What a picture: a mother stirring a kettle of yellow lentils while balancing an undiapered baby on her hip. It mattered not that the color of the lentils resembled the discharge from the baby. Plates were limited so the guests ate in turn, two and three eating off the same plates washed by the rain. The older children braved the storm to pick up the broken branches to be used later for fuel. Some picked up fallen mangoes which they shared with all. They took turns sleeping where they sat. The second day the sun came out and so did all the soaked bedding to be dried in the sun. The mud floors were repaired and allowed to dry before the roof was restored. And life went on.

During one of the worst floods while we were living in Gopalganj, our house, one of the highest points in the village, was surrounded by water. Our small boat, tied to the porch post, was used to travel from house to house to visit and pray with the people. The boat, in many cases could enter right inside the house where the family was sitting on the large plank bed elevated with bricks.

When strong winds and rain continued over a period of time the hard clay floors of the houses were soon reduced to mud and loosened posts that held up the grass roofs would collapse. As flood waters rose many ran for the trees. We visited a family living on a platform in a large tree near our house. To reach them we walked up to our knees in muddy water and refuse from outside toilets. After climbing a makeshift ladder to the platform we sat talking and praying with the family. I still cannot explain where they got clear water to wash our feet and legs. I was overwhelmed by their hospitality.

It had rained for many days and the already saturated earth could not drink any more. I stood on the porch watching Calvin and another man trying to get water from the community pump before it was swallowed up in the flood waters. Having filled a washtub with water, the were returning home in a canoe-like boat. Suddenly the boat capsized before my eyes with tub, Calvin, and camera. The first words I yelled, which Calvin would never let me forget, were, "Be careful of the camera!" But it was too late. The camera was ruined, Calvin lost his shoes and the tub was stuck in the mud at the bottom of the flood waters. The diary does not tell me what water we drank after that. We offered one dollar, a day's wage at that time, to anyone who would retrieve the aluminum tub. It was returned that day.

Since there was no dry land in which to bury the dead, bricks were tied to the deceased so they would sink in the flood water. In some cases the bricks sank without the bodies and we watched the bloated corpses float past our house and out into the open country. The village tube well pump was submerged for days and the flood water was polluted resulting in the death of many, especially children.

Riots

The two week evangelism tour in several villages had been completed and we were on our way home. Lying on bamboo mats under the low round roof of a hired boat we tried to relax. The Muslim boatman sitting on the pointed end of the craft slowly poled us through canal after canal and finally a river. We were suddenly aroused by excited shouts of men which became louder as they drew closer. Our boatman yelled for us to lie down and not show our faces, while he continued to pole the boat. When the shouting men carrying knives and machetes inquired through the darkness, "Who's there?" the boatman replied. "We are all Muslims. Do us no harm, we are just traveling home." Seemingly convinced, the Muslim men moved on raising their voices again in a war cry.

The riots became widespread and we found our house in Gopalganj surrounded with people banging on the doors and windows. Much to our relief we found not rioters but innocent people who were fleeing for protection. How many could three rooms hold? We decided to give refuge to the women and children and let the men serve as watchmen of the village. We laid out mats on the floor but there was no sleep that night. We could hear the roar of human voices as throngs of people rushed through the streets shouting slogans and waving banners and brandishing bamboo sticks. Any opposition meant conflict.

The next day we could see smoke rising from burning villages. We learned later that the trouble began when Muslims let their cattle graze in a Hindu rice field. Our immediate area was not affected so our overnight guests returned to find their houses intact. Similar riots in the past were precipitated when a Hindu's obnoxious pig wandered onto Muslim territory, or the Muslims would butcher a cow in full view of Hindu neighbors, who considered the cow most sacred.

The riot could have continued for days but a severe storm with hurricane winds brought an end to the conflict as people were distracted by flying debris. Again our house was crowded as the wind and rain caused roofs to collapse. We were anxious at times when our tin roof seemed to rise and fall under the force of the wind. The bolts loosened but held.

Soon reports came of a distant Christian village that had been burned and the people were calling for Calvin's help. He made plans to go immediately. It was an eight hour trip by boat. I was left alone. People fleeing their burning villages became refugees in our town. Everyone rallied to help. I could hear women and children weeping as they paraded past our house carrying their few remaining possessions. Eleven Christian men from the village where Calvin had gone marched into our town chained to each other as they were led to the local prison. Separated by many hours from Calvin I felt rather insecure.

After four days Calvin returned, covered with mud and suffering from boils. After a shower he went immediately to check on the Christian prisoners. He recognized one of the men but could not speak to him. From then on he made daily trips and eventually was able to visit with the men. It took weeks to clear the case and the men were freed. We still do not know why they were arrested, nor do they.

One time during such riots we witnessed the burning of an entire village. The following day we walked through that village to find only scattered grains of rice mixed with straw from the roofs of the houses. The only signs of life were the stray dogs and cats searching for food. Smoke still rose from the smoldering embers. Such was the display of the violent side of the Bengali people. A whole new village would appear within weeks. I have never known such resilience as displayed by the people of Bangladesh.

Chapter Twenty-Two

Travel
"In journeyings often, in perils of waters…"
–2 Corinthians 11:26, KJV

It was quite an adventure to travel from Gopalganj, the village where we lived for six years, to the closest city, Khulna, for necessities like sugar, flour, banking and postage. To get from our house to the launch dock usually took one hour by a small boat. Since night travel was not safe we always planned to arrive at the dock before dark.

We would go to the riverside where the small boats are lined up and choose a boatman whose boat did not leak. The choice is important as one trusts his life to a stranger, traveling in the dark through the murky waters and tall grass smothering the river. For one hour we would sit cross legged, surrounded by our luggage under the low roof of the canoe-like boat. The glow of kerosene lanterns of the tiny riverside tea shops were a welcoming sight. Along with others we would wait for hours for the "never on time" launches.

During the waiting time we would often spread out our bed rolls on the floating docks and try to sleep. On one particular trip as we nestled down we were distracted by the motion of the moving dock, the falling dew that penetrated our sleeping bags, and also the loud voices of men nearby. Not realizing we could understand every word they said in their language one man proceeded to tell the others what the white man eats, and how he uses a fork; how he talks; the kind of house he lives in; the dog whose bark can be heard a mile away; and the large white box in the white man's house that has a door on hinges which is heated by kerosene and freezes water into little cubes. Hearing the sound of the approaching launch we hastened to roll up our bedding. Calvin greeted the men in the Bengali language. You should have seen their eyes.

After a severe storm when the winds reached 150 mph many riverboats were damaged and launch and steamer service was disrupted. We had steamer reservations for the trip to the port city of Chittagong where we were scheduled for meetings at the church. We heard that the steamers were not running. From a distance of two miles one could usually hear the steamer horn as it arrived and left the docks. We could not send a telegram nor phone a message. We waited two more days then decided to chance it. I had baked fresh bread for the trip as there was none available in the market. Usually we took homemade peanut butter and fresh fruit when we traveled. The next morning we hired a small boat to take us and our luggage to the steamer dock. Arriving after a two hour trip through canals to the big river, we discovered that a steamer, the first in four days, had just departed. It was twelve noon and the next steamer would arrive at 5:30 the next morning.

We decided to wait at the docks along with many other passengers. We took shelter from the sun and ate our lunch in a nearby empty hut while sitting on a wooden bed. After an hour's sleep we bought rice and some dried lentils from a small shop and the boatman who had brought us offered to cook us a meal in his boat. I watched him remove a couple of small boards in the boat floor and pull out a portable clay stove, some firewood, and a cooking pot. In no time we had hot rice with curry spiced lentils (dal) which we shared with him.

Sleeping was not easy. By now the wooden bed in the shack was occupied so we spread out our bedding rolls on the ground with our heads just under the eaves of the building for protection from the heavy dew. We slept until we heard the horn of the approaching steamer at 5 a.m.

Our reservations had expired and there was no vacant cabin. We sat in the boat's dining room until the afternoon when two Anglican priests disembarked at Barisal. While I guarded our luggage in the now empty cabin, Calvin sent a telegram informing the Chittagong pastor of our delay. Day trips on steamers are hot, very hot. Every available space on deck was covered with people and luggage. The cabins are small with a ceiling fan that circulates the one hundred degree air. But we were thankful for the privacy and a place to sit and lie down.

After a day and night on the steamer we arrived at Chandpur town, transferred to a train which would take us the remaining eight hours to our destination. No one met us, and no one received our telegram.

Security is a luxury we take for granted at times. Traveling on a steamer you can never be sure the door to your cabin is locked. If it is locked there are ways to unlock it without a key. Sleep does not come easy. Most of the passengers are sleeping on the boards of the open deck so thievery is quite common. On one trip in the middle of the night a boy traveling first class in a cabin yelled out that his money bag was missing. People began accusing each other. Rumors spread and ended when one man slapped another five times in the face because he called him "Shallah," brother-in-law (wife's brother), which doubles as a curse word. The thief was never caught and few got sleep that night.

Chapter Twenty-Three

Bridges and Gangplanks
"The greatest risk is not to take one."
–Unknown

L ooking back now on travel in Bangladesh I wonder how I managed. At first I gazed in awe mixed with fear at the one bamboo bridge stretched across a canal. Bamboo bridges have always been a challenge. They come in all lengths stretching over short and long spans of water. The bamboos may be thin or stout. They may or may not have a railing of one bamboo also. On one occasion, with the absence of a railing we used a stray bamboo pole for balance. We would thrust it in the mud at the canal's bottom at intervals to steady ourselves. If you are fortunate there may be two bamboos on which to place your feet. The weight of your body causes the pole to bend, often within inches of the water. If several people attempt to cross the bridge at the same time it is important "to keep in step" with the same gait and speed. When it rains, or early in the morning when the dew has not yet evaporated, the bridge is slippery. I believe the people of Bangladesh are born with a great sense of balance. I was not.

Just outside one village we came upon a canal with a single bamboo pole bridge now slippery from the rain and with no railing. Calvin picked up the loose pole lying on the bank and with sure steps crossed first. He then threw the pole back to me. When I refused to cross because of fear he let me know he was continuing on without me if necessary. I somehow managed and on the opposite shore pulled myself up the slippery muddy bank by grabbing the bare roots of a tree. I was glad for the rain that washed my clothes and I arrived at our destination clean though wet.

Once when Calvin attempted to carry his motorbike across such a bridge he decided it was cheaper and safer to hire a man and his boat to paddle or pole him to his destination. In a country of numerous waterways this was feasible. As I recall the bamboo bridges in my life I can think of only one mishap. I dropped my umbrella midstream and a man taking his daily bath retrieved it for me.

Boarding a launch or river steamer was not too difficult if there was a regular boat landing. However, disembarking in the villages without the luxury of a dock, one walked gingerly down a plank with a wobbly bamboo railing. Often the gangplank did not quite reach the shore so you were deposited in ankle deep water to wade the rest of the way. In some situations there was still the muddy bank to conquer. It is an advantage to travel shoeless.

I remember disembarking from a launch at Haridashpur, the closest stop to our village, when the gang plank ended in mud. Since the canal to our village was too shallow for boats to navigate we had to walk the rest of the way. With shoes in hand we proceeded barefoot stepping over fresh human droppings. Reaching dry terrain we sat on a tree stump with legs dangling while we waited for some boys to fetch river water to wash our feet. From there the remaining trip was by foot over rough terrain. During the rainy season one's foot prints dig deep into the mud which become hard as rock as soon as the sun beats down on them. We eventually caught up with the hired men who had walked on ahead carrying our luggage.

Calvin often traveled with co-worker, Orville Carlson. Once in a small Speed The Light launch with outboard motor the two of them journeyed to a distant village. Suddenly a freak storm arose making motoring impossible so they tied up to a tree at the bank to wait out the storm. While they were napping the storm subsided and the tide retreated, leaving the boat and men stuck on a sand bar. It meant waiting out the tide as well.

On another occasion as Calvin pulled the cord to start the tiny motor on our small aluminum boat he saw a live snake entwined in the motor. This caused quite a stir as the crowd gathered to watch this white man tackle a black snake. Travel was never easy nor did it lack excitement.

Chapter Twenty-Four

Foot Paths
*"He who chooses a path,
chooses also it's destination."*
–Unknown

In the small town where we lived there were no roads. The main thoroughfare through the town was about six feet wide, just enough room for people to pass. Dirt paths leading out of the town were half as wide. Usually people walked single file, women always behind the men. Often these paths were built up higher than the adjoining rice fields. They became slippery and muddy when wet, and hard as brick when dry.

From my window I have watched women traveling home from the well carrying a jug on one hip and a baby on the other. Men returning from the area market carried produce in baskets on their heads. Bails of freshly cut rice stalks tied to either end of a pole are balanced on the shoulders of men headed for the threshing floor.

Rain or shine, with or without an umbrella, they walk. It is a familiar gait never missing a beat. No one minds the rain in the tropics. It brings relief from the heat. One revels in the wet, clear water running over the body leaving a feeling of a hot tub bath. When the rain stops and the sun shines your wet clothes soon dry. I have watched naked children with faces upturned toward the sky singing as they run to and fro in the rain, reveling in its wetness. Cupping their hands they collected drops for a drink. I can see where Rabindranath Tagore, the famous Bengali poet got inspiration for his poems.

Let me describe one trip. We had already traveled all day in a small boat, crouched under the low curved roof made of bamboo matting. For a change in position we would sometimes walk along the bank of the canal shielded by umbrellas. Having traveled as far as we could by boat, we hired a man to carry our luggage and we began our two mile hike to Suogram village.

By now it was raining and our clothes were soon soaked in spite of umbrellas. The wind was blowing and our feet made a crunching sound as we stepped on fallen branches from the many palm trees. Suddenly I felt a severe pain in one toe. Upon examination we discovered I had stepped on a thorny branch from the date palm tree and one of the two inch long needle-like thorns had pierced my leather shoe, nailing a toe to the inner sole. No way could we extricate it except to force the shoe off by breaking the thorn. This would cause immediate swelling of the foot. Since we still had another hour to walk we decided to wait until we reached our destination.

We arrived weary, dirty, and in pain at the pastor's one room, thatched roofed house. First of all we had to remove the thorn. As Calvin, with force, removed the shoe I proceeded to faint. Now they were all in trouble since the only nurse within many miles was unconscious. We had an extended stay with the family waiting for the swelling to subside enough to wear a shoe. Nights were spent lying on a platform of split bamboos in a lean-to shed attached to the house. There was little sleep for me due to pain and sounds of baby goats under our bed calling for their mother in another part of the shed. The Hindus were celebrating some religious holiday as they chanted prayers all night to their many gods. At dawn the rooster, also under our bed, announced it was time to get up. Even without medication there was no infection. The foot healed sufficiently so that within three days I was able to continue the tour.

Chapter Twenty-Five

Rest Rooms and I
"Rest is simply release!"
–A. W. Tozer

Most "outdoor toilets" in Bangladesh are roofless. I recall in the middle of the night sliding off a board bed and walking to the edge of the jungle to relieve myself. With the flashlight in one hand and fanning off mosquitoes and other insects with the other hand I could only pray that no snakes, red biting ants or leeches would discover me. There have been times when I have told my body it does not need relief as I lacked courage to use the "facility."

Calvin tells of the time he was preaching in a village church, the frame of which was bamboo with wooden pillars. Suddenly a northwest storm hit with strong winds and rain. The men ran for the pillars to hold them in place, for once the mud floor softened the roof would collapse. Later, in the same building, Calvin climbed a bamboo ladder to the loft which served as a guest room. In the middle of the night he was awakened by cramps and the urge to visit the outhouse. Climbing down the ladder he proceeded with a flashlight in one hand and an umbrella in the other.

Rain from above and mud beneath made walking

difficult. Even more treacherous was the slanting bamboo ramp leading up to the outhouse which was a bamboo structure over a marsh. Once inside the burlap walls he had to balance in a squatting position on two bamboo poles, now wet and slippery, about a foot apart. Due to diarrhea he had to make that trip several times that night. There was little sleep and there would be no sleep the next day as he would be traveling to another village.

When traveling to other cultures it is important early on to learn the name for what we call the "Rest Room" in the American culture. We should know if it is called latrine, outhouse, lavatory, washroom, rest room, john, pykhana ghar, pit stop, little room, ladies room, powder room, W.C. (water closet), loo, toilette, biffy or "I want to spend a penny" (a common English colloquialism).

Also it takes time to figure out the name attached to the toilet doors. There are labels for unisex, male or female, or no name at all with only figures that look like a man or a woman and whose figures change with cultures. A long skirt may mean a man while pants may mean a woman. Experiment brings proof.

We can no longer call the seat a stool as it may only be a hole in the floor or ground or two bamboo poles on which to balance over a marsh. To leave the facility clean one must figure out if you need to pull a chain, step on a pedal, push a button, jiggle a handle, or push a detonator on the back of the commode and then quickly exit before it overflows; or in the case of an "outhouse," just walk away and leave it to nature.

Most rest rooms in the world are free. In one middle eastern country the rest room was guarded by an old woman sitting at a makeshift table who pushed a cardboard box toward you with a slit in the lid. No set charge. Give what you can or desire. I guess it depends on how bad you need the facility and how long you can hold your breath. In this incident there was no paper, soap, or water.

I remember the time in a foreign airport when I was chased up a long flight of steps by a shouting woman, angry because I had not tipped her in the rest room. I had failed to communicate with my hands that I had no local currency. She waited while I collected some coins from Calvin. In Europe more than once I was delayed as I sought for the proper coin to enter the stall. There are times, in spite of odor or hygiene, when you're willing to pay any amount to use a toilet which you wouldn't go within a mile of at home.

And then there is the traveler to our own United States of America who finds the rest room locked and the key must be requested. The seat that flips up and down, is usually soiled, flushers don't flush, and there is limited space to close the door without losing one's balance. When one is unable to identify the pant clad leg in the next booth panic sets in.

The Asian toilet, to which I eventually adapted and preferred, is a sunken commode with the rim even with the floor and a tiny raised platform on either side large enough for your feet to rest. You don't stand but squat over the hole. There is nothing to hold on to and even if there was, there would be no free hand to grab it as your arms are full of skirts and miscellaneous as you protect them from the environment, especially the puddles on the floor. Someone has said that "You've been in Asia too long if the foot prints on your American toilet seat are your own."

The Bangladesh "outhouse," common in the villages, is perched on stilts, 6 to 10 feet above a swamp connected to dry ground by a bamboo ladder. Walls and door are flapping burlap sacks attached to a bamboo frame. If the occupant is standing he can easily be identified. One straddles or rather balances on two bamboo poles placed horizontally two feet apart. On a rainy day the roofless structure and slippery bamboo makes life miserable.

You could always identify visitors to the village outhouse by their little jug. Each person would carry a pitcher of water, their substitute for toilet tissue. Holding the jug in the right hand it would be tilted while the left hand was free to cleanse the designated area with the flowing water. This explains why one is permitted to eat with the right hand only. A child soon learns to reserve the left hand for the bathroom and always give and receive with the right hand.

It is not uncommon to see men squatting along the roadside in some countries in Asia. But I have never seen a woman squat in public. Someone said they only relieve themselves after sunset and before sunrise. I recall seeing shadows groping through the high grain in the fields or down on the banks of the canal at twilight or predawn. I was sure it was the women.

Mother's anticipate their babies and toddlers' needs and will hold the child over a positioned banana leaf on the ground. The leaf will then be deposited in the outside toilet.

The old American "outhouse" is not too bad after all! I've just thought of some little miracles: I have never fallen in a hole; never contracted a venereal disease; never dropped valuables; never fainted; and never met one of the opposite sex in all my adventures.

I must add I have not experienced the toilet in space. They tell me it provides a seat belt and head and feet restraints. Whether the color-matched-cushioned stool in America, or the spot in the jungle with the starry sky as roof, it's still a toilet.

Post script: Next to my passport, American toilet paper is my most treasured traveling companion.

Chapter Twenty-Six

Miracles
*"One can have expectation without faith,
but you cannot have faith without expectation."*
–Marian N. Olson

One day Mrs. Haldar brought her husband to our home just as we sat down to eat breakfast. We heard coughing at our door and knew that someone had arrived. I soon discovered the cough was not to announce their arrival but the indication of something medically very serious. He was too weak to stand on his own as he leaned heavily on his wife. The wife reported that the doctor said he would die of tuberculosis within a month. As we sat in the usual manner on mats spread on the cement floor we prayed that his spiritual eyes would be opened and he would understand God's plan of salvation. He prayed the sinner's prayer and light spread across his face. We then prayed for his healing and he experienced a measure of relief as he stood up and with the help of his wife walked away. We heard nothing more. Two weeks later Calvin went to the river bank to arrange for a boatman to take him to a village six hours away. While bargaining with one boatman another man came running up yelling, "Sir, I will take you, hire me." Turning in his direction, Calvin could not believe what he saw. It was the TB patient. Immediately Calvin rejected him with these words. "I need to get to my destination today and no way could you paddle that distance." But the man insisted that Jesus had healed him. And he was right. The man who was to die within a month rowed and poled Calvin for six hours in the hot sun. We saw him ten years later still serving as a boatman and serving the Lord.

Peering out the window I saw a figure entering our gate, covered completely with a black cotton robe except for two net-covered holes for the eyes. This one was for me, I said to myself. Calvin disappeared as I invited the woman inside where we sat cross-legged on woven bamboo mats spread on the cement floor. We were alone. She lifted the flap of cloth concealing her face, revealing an expression of pain and hopelessness.

She had heard that we prayed for her Christian neighbor's son whose fever immediately disappeared and he ran outside to play. This 26 year old Muslim woman, mother of nine children, had come requesting prayer for herself. Due to the stresses of poverty, large family, overwork, husband's unemployment, and physical weakness from bearing a child every year, she had become depressed. Repeatedly beating the top of her head with an iron pipe she had tried to kill herself. She did not die. She lived with unbearable pain, day and night. Could our God heal her? Speaking in her language I described Jesus as Savior of the world who FORGIVES sin, HEALS our sicknesses, and gives us

PEACE while we live on earth and gives us HOPE of Heaven when we die. These were four blessings her religion could not give her. After prayer she lifted her face, wreathed in smiles. "It works!" she exclaimed. "Already I feel better." I watched her as she covered her face and walked rapidly down the path toward home. Would she come back?

Several days later she did return, this time with her husband, to give thanks to Jesus who healed her. We presented them with a New Testament in their language and prayed that the truth of God's Word would penetrate their hearts and have an effect on their lives. They walked away believing.

Sultana's entire body was still draped with a black robe, but the veil of her heart had been lifted.

Chitta Bala, a Christian from a nearby village, arrived one morning at our home with his seven year old son. We soon learned the boy was born deaf. This meant he could not attend school. Sign language was completely foreign to them. This was their only son and their future security. Their daughters would marry and leave home. The son would always stay with the parents. Who would want to marry a deaf mute? Who would care for him after his parents were gone? We listened to this father spill out his pent up feelings. I knew that unless God performed a miracle this child would always be deaf.

This was a challenge! After praying for the child and encouraging the father we parted. We stood on the porch and watched as father and son walked out of the gate and down the lane. We felt their pain.

A week or so later they returned with the good news that the boy was responding to sounds and trying to talk. In time that little boy's hearing became perfectly normal. He was able to attend school and today he pastors a church. They not only experienced a miracle but also came to know the God of miracles.

Chapter Twenty-Seven

Demons
*"What's happening is not really
what's going on."*
–Anonymous

Calvin had been on a preaching tour in the village for two weeks. The plan was for me to meet him on a certain date in Chorkhuli (Thieves village). Since it would be improper for me to travel alone, I took the pastor's eleven year old daughter with me. It took us more than eight hours to go sixteen miles in a small boat. If only there had been a dry path we could have walked it much faster. Calvin had arrived at the planned rendezvous just thirty minutes before us.

The local pastor arranged for us to stay in a one room thatched roof house owned by a widow who had gone to a distant city for a visit. This hut was located about the distance of a city block from the Pastor's house where we went for each meal and about two blocks from the church. The edge of the jungle, which was the public toilet, was about 50 yards away.

We were warned at once by neighbors that we should never leave our clothes and bedding unwatched day or night as the place was frequented by thieves. While we went to meals one of the neighbor women guarded the house. While I was having women's or children's meetings in the afternoon Calvin would stay in the house. While he preached at night in the church I "stayed by the stuff."

It happened the last night we were there. It was 11 p.m. Sunday. Calvin had come home from the night service and was preparing to retire when the pastor called him to go pray for a demon possessed girl, a young bride, in the next village about a mile away.

The owner of the house where we were staying and her fourteen year old son had arrived home that day. They insisted on sleeping on the open porch under a mosquito net. The woman went with the two men to pray for the girl, leaving the boy asleep on the porch and I inside the house on a folding cot, protected by a mosquito net.

The door was my height, made of dried reeds fastened together with jute string and was placed to one side during the day and tied in place during the night. Neither the reed walls or door reached to the slanting grass roof so it was easy for someone to take anything within reach. We were careful not to hang anything close to the walls.

After midnight I was awakened from a deep sleep and perceived a presence in the room and it wasn't Calvin. It was total darkness and Calvin had taken the flashlight with him. I had placed the door in position without tying it so Calvin could easily enter without my crawling out from under the mosquito net. My first thought was that a cat had entered the room or a thief. I was petrified and could not move but I instinctively screamed "chor, chor" the word "thief" in the Bengali language. There was no reply.

There was a shuffling sound inside the hut as the

shouting neighbors came running with a kerosene lantern. A runner was sent to inform Calvin that his wife was in danger. Whoever had entered my room escaped, knocking down the door and ripping the mosquito net which covered the boy sleeping on the porch. The neighbors, all talking at once, had now entered the little hut. The boy had awakened but was too frightened to move. I still had not risen from my cot but began to repeat the name of Jesus and pray for protection.

When Calvin arrived I had calmed down and could talk. Relieved to find me safe, he told of the girl's deliverance. The demons spoke through her in a very rough voice giving their names and said they came from a house which was the one right next to the hut where I was sleeping. When the demons left the girl they threatened to leave a sign. We were convinced it was not a thief that had visited me but it was the "sign" the demons mentioned. The reed door of the hut was forced into the rafters in a way that no human could have manipulated.

Then Calvin described the evening's episode. He had found the young bride scratching the walls of the little hut with both hands, hair disheveled, clothing torn, speaking in a rough male voice. Everyone was asked to leave the room except the husband of the girl and the pastor. For two hours they prayed, talked to the demons who said they would go but would leave a sign. Then they would change their minds and not go. This was repeated several times.

Suddenly Calvin began to sing "There is Power in the Blood of Jesus." The demons in the girl began to scream and instantly she fell down on the floor as though dead. There was no movement. Calvin bent over her and whispered in her ear, "Say the name of Jesus." Only her lips moved. He told her to say it louder. Then faintly a sound could be heard which gradually increased in volume as she said the name of Jesus. Immediately she sat up. She was completely healed. Calvin then explained to her about the power of Jesus' blood to forgive sins. Right there she repeated the sinner's prayer.

The following morning on our way to another village we stopped by to see the new bride who had been delivered the night before. She had bathed, was wearing a clean sari, and served us tea and toast. Again God's power had prevailed.

Chapter Twenty-Eight

Cholera Epidemic – 1964
"Weeping in the Banana Grove"

Each year, on April 24, I celebrate the anniversary of one of God's great miracles. It was dusk in Bangladesh. The air was thick with smoke from damp wood and cow dung fires mixed with the pungent odors of spices cooking for the evening meal. Children huddled close to home while the sound of weeping could be heard through the banana grove adjacent to our home. The dreaded disease, cholera, stalked the village.

The day had been hot, humid, and exhausting. The call for help had come at dawn and I quickly joined others who labored to save lives. We wept with the living as we saw through the trees the mounds of fresh earth in the nearby field. We had watched for hours the wasting forms lying on woven mats on the mud floors – voiceless, pale, and hopeless.

One hut sheltered a mother of six, lying on the floor with her long black hair spread behind her on a banana leaf. A neighbor poured water steadily over the fevered brow. A narrow shallow trench encircling the body drained off water and refuse, while seven pairs of fearful eyes watched mother and wife die.

A grandmother grabbed my hand. She led me to a child with skin drawn tightly over protruding bones and body twitching from muscle spasms, the last stage of cholera. "Where is his mother?" I whispered. The old woman pointed with her chin toward the mounds of earth. This was the third in one family.

Cholera spread rapidly through the villages. Flies would carry the disease from neighbor to neighbor. In five hours a person could die if fluids lost through vomiting and diarrhea were not immediately replaced. Unfortunately in this epidemic there was no such life saving facilities. I visited from house to house trying to save some. Today I buried a whole family in one grave. The risk was great. Tomorrow I could die.

The time had come for our annual release from work, a two weeks' vacation. Exhausted from sleepless, hot nights with no electricity, and from days of trying to curb the cholera epidemic in 100 degree temperatures we were ready for a change. Two days later, packed in a bus with hot and sticky people and bundles of bedding, we journeyed north to Shillong, a hilly country of North East India. We welcomed a hot bath and the shelter in a guest room of the nurses' residence of the Welch Presbyterian Mission Hospital. The very first night I was awakened at 2 a.m. with the familiar symptoms of cholera. The vomiting and diarrhea continued for five hours. Not wanting to disturb the nursing staff before 7 a.m. we delayed calling for help.

I was becoming weaker and dehydration of nose and mouth made breathing difficult. The skin was dry and tongue relaxed as there was no saliva to swallow, and no water for tears. Muscle pains and convulsions would follow and the struggle would be short. When the doctors tried to inject fluid they found the veins had collapsed. Just before losing consciousness I faintly heard Calvin's voice which seemed to mingle with others weeping in the banana grove. He prayed, "Lord alert someone else to pray for Marian as I can no longer pray."

The setting had changed but the hour was the same. Sweeping 10,000 miles westward across many time zones it was now 3:30 p.m., April 24, 1962, in rural Easton, Pennsylvania. The local Women's Ministries group had gathered at the church for prayer and work. They were talking informally while sewing. Suddenly a soft spoken lady uttered a sound of despair as she exclaimed, "Pray for the Olsons; they are in danger." The Holy Spirit had alerted this intercessor to our need. The ladies joined her in prayer. They wept, pleaded, and groaned in the spirit for a need they could not describe. Rising to her feet 2 hours later, Mrs. Roger Templeton wiped away the tears and announced, "It's all right now."

And it was all right! Halfway around the globe I opened my eyes to a world of white figures, quiet voices and a half-empty bottle hanging above me releasing life giving glucose through a needle into my vein. I was breathing and swallowing again. Death had been cheated. The following day I was walking and eating normally. What if Mrs. Templeton had missed her cue or had not instantly responded. Her intercessory prayer had released God's power and I am alive today. I am reminded that "The prayer of a righteous man (woman) is powerful and effective" (James 5:16, NIV).

Gopalganj

Olson's
village
residence

Private boat landing
at Olson's house

Olson's house
during flood

Village scene –
rice fields

Children
fishing

Man carrying
bundles of rice

Traveling by
boat, 1957

Traveling by
boat, 1999

Local instruments –
harmonium and
drum (tabla)

Boarding
a launch

Laundry man
with donkey

Village toilet (outhouse)

Crossing bamboo bridge

Calvin shaving
during village tour

Calvin
pushing
boat into
river

Marian fell
on a muddy
path

Shoes
outside
of church
entrance

East Pakistan
before
Civil War,
1971

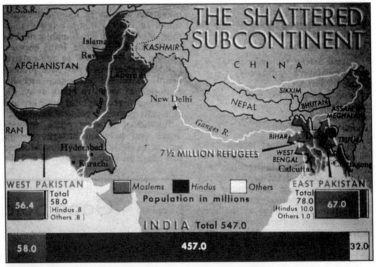

Bangladesh born, 1971

PART THREE
Dhaka

An Island in a sea of villages
Winding concrete paths
Grass huts in the shadow of
Multi-storied dwellings
Barred windows, flat roofs
Flowers, flute, children
Crows, dogs, and beggars
A home for nine million.

–Marian N. Olson

Chapter Twenty-Nine

A Church Is Born
"God waits to be wanted."
–A. W. Tozer

U ntil 1962 there was no A. G. Church in Dhaka, the capital city. Ruth and Don Tarno, newly appointed A.G. missionaries, started a Bible study in the home of a British couple, Mr. and Mrs. Eachus, who were living in Dhaka. I joined Ruth in conducting a week of Bible Classes for children which brought us in touch with their parents.

Two years later Don and Ruth opened a Christian bookstore on Jinnah Avenue, in the "center of the city." Eventually a small group of Christians who understood English met in part of the store for Sunday services. Several miracles of healing at that time attracted others.

As the attendance increased there were some who requested a service in their mother tongue. The time seemed ripe to begin meetings in the Bengali language. Calvin and I were invited to join the Tarnos for several weeks in a special effort to organize such a group. This was the beginning of what is now Bethel Church of the Assembly of God Church Center located on New Eskaton Road.

It was during this time, April 1964, that Calvin began

a forty day fast while we were still guests in the Tarno home. With the arrival of the Muslim holiday Eid, Calvin and I traveled by rickshaw (an adult size tricycle with a seat for two built over the two back wheels) through the old city of Dhaka. We wanted to observe and take pictures of the slaughter of animals to commemorate Abraham's offering of Isaac (or Ishmael as Muslims believe).

When we arrived back at Tarno's house God asked Calvin if he was a tourist or a missionary. Calvin replied that he was a tourist today taking pictures. God impressed upon him to return to that very market place the next day with the message that Jesus had made the final sacrifice for our sins.

The next day at 4 p.m. Calvin made his way back to the same area to some of the same people. The day before they were amazed he could speak their language and invited him to return. This day when he handed them a tract and explained about Jesus' sacrifice for our sins they were not so pleasant. In fact they told him not to come back again.

Each day he would awaken with the urge to return to the market place though his flesh rebelled. He thought each trip was the last but it continued for 40 days throughout the fast. He was spit upon; had yellow coloring thrown on his clothing; was pushed into the drains, which are used as toilets; and one time even locked up in a small shop.

One day they invited him to a debate with three Muslims. After they had presented their beliefs, Calvin asked two questions. Do you know your sins are forgiven? Do you know when you die, you will go to heaven? Their answer was no to both. With great confidence he gave them his testimony and the assurance he had that his sins were forgiven and one day he would go to Heaven. The debate was over and Calvin left. In spite of the opposition he knew he had to return.

As he was distributing tracts on one visit, a Muslim priest dressed in a white robe and white cap pushed his way through the crowd, grabbed Calvin's shoulder bag of tracts and threw the leaflets into the air. Taking one in his hand he waved it in front of the crowd with these words, "Everyone take a paper, read it. We'll all become Christian and dance naked in the streets." Apparently American TV had reached them first.

Always surrounded by a crowd on his visits, he knew if they became violent there was no way of escape. Don Tarno, realized Calvin was getting weaker from the fast so insisted on going with him the 39th day. It was on that day they approached him with clubs and threatened to kill him if he returned one more time.

In the meantime they arranged for a group of university students to be present the next day. Calvin prayed that God would release him from those daily trips but the following morning, day number 40, he knew he had to go and face the angry mob. He kissed me goodbye realizing he might never see me again. I watched him walk alone out of the house and board a rickshaw. The next two hours I walked the floor in tear-drenched prayer.

They were ready for him when he arrived at the regular meeting place. The angry students and hundreds of others cried "We want blood!" They pushed him, pummeled him with their fists, and could have trampled him underfoot.

At the most crucial time when he expected that any moment could be his last, two tall men pushed their way through the crowd toward him. Taking him by the arms, one on either side, they forced their way through the cheering crowd. Calvin thought it was all over. They will take me down some alley, finish me off and Marian will never find me. Instead, the two men walked with him to a waiting rickshaw, helped him up on the seat and said, "It is enough for now. Don't come back here any more." And the two men disappeared. Not one person from the crowd moved toward him. We knew immediately that God had sent his angels.

By now he was so weak from fasting he could hardly walk. At night neither of us could sleep. I had walked the floor, praying, during the two hours from 5 to 7 p.m. each evening when he was walking the streets of the market place. Suffering from anxiety I had problems eating and sleeping. Our colleagues encouraged Cal to discontinue the fast. When a telegram from head-quarters, U.S.A., arrived with the request that Calvin terminate the fast he submitted. Gradually his strength returned and he suffered no permanent effects from the long fast. There is a church located in that area today.

Chapter Thirty

New Assignment
*"Every job is the self portrait
of the person who did it."*
–Anonymous

F ive years later, in 1969 we were transferred from Gopalganj to Dhaka where Calvin spent the next twenty-one years as pastor of the English congregation and assistant to the Bengali pastor of the vernacular church.

Life was somewhat easier in Dhaka with running water and electricity, but there were new adjustments. Anti-American, anti-missionary feelings were strong. One day we came upon a slogan written in English in large letters on a white wall, "Missionary go home." We were not wanted or appreciated by the rich and powerful political society of the big city.

I was not prepared for the city noise, the sounds of heavy traffic with constant use of air horns, noisy crows fighting at the garbage heaps and people shouting as they bargained from shop to shop. Then there were the odors of stale food, open drains used as public toilets, exhaust from the leaded fuel used by most vehicles, and wood smoke from homes and shops. Walking became a chore as I picked my way among the wandering chickens, goats and dogs, and detoured around the neighborhood dump. Often I longed for the quieter, cleaner village life.

Half the people in Dhaka, (now ten million), live below the poverty line with one-third of that number considered slum dwellers. It is not surprising that about half of the people are ill at any given time when you consider that about half of the cities population has no access to sanitary latrines. Since most of the people in Bangladesh have been poor for generations, poverty increases with the ever growing population. Fifty percent of the 130 million people go to bed hungry.

In a Muslim country where most women were not seen on the streets unveiled, my life style took on another change. Living in a rented apartment next to the church I found my world consisted of these few hundred square feet, looking at the world through barred windows. With isolation, loss of privacy, and lack of mental stimulation how could I share with others my joy and discovery of peace with God? How could I reach them on their level, sit where they sit, think what they think, talk their language, feel what they feel? What did we have in common?

Soon curious neighbors came to see the white lady with brown hair, blue eyes, and soft skin. They walked freely through our apartment, opening and closing doors and drawers while amazed looks spread across their faces. Then they invited me to visit their humble abodes of one or two rooms, a galvanized tin roof, and tin or brick walls.

I observed how the Bengali people with their "open house policy," shared the family bed with guests at night, served everyone tea, borrowed from neighbors to feed unexpected visitors, and spent countless hours talking. They taught me how to serve and share all I have. It was then I discovered the ministry of hospitality.

Oh there were meetings with women and children in the Sunday school and church, but my mission to the UNREACHED was in my home. They would come out of curiosity and go away with tea and a prayer.

Chapter Thirty-One

The Bug...Twice Bought
*"Silver trumpets are apt to be
a great snare to their owner who wastes
much time in polishing them."*
–Zelma Argue

Now that we were living in the city we were assigned our first car. The Assembly of God youth, through a project known as "Speed the Light," had raised the money for this vehicle. It was a Volkswagen, popularly known as "the Bug." Ordered from Germany and received at the Chittagong docks in Bangladesh, it became ours in 1968 after paying 100 percent duty. It was paid for twice.

The manual says it will seat four. We have seen eleven children packed in the back seat and the storage area behind the seat while four sat in front. The culture enjoyed closeness and did not require the space bubble of most Americans. It was not equipped with seat belts. The VW's size allowed us to travel down narrow lanes where many of our Christians lived. There were many of its kind as small cars were more common at that time. Immediately we had a rack installed on the roof. This was not only handy for carrying luggage when we traveled to remote areas but also for "Light for the Lost

Literature" which we freely distributed.

The Bug has its own diary. Often it was covered with mud while traveling on dirt roads during the monsoon (rainy season) but then washed clean again by a sudden heavy shower. It became used to the crowds that would hug its sides and tap on the windows during village trips. We had to creep inch by inch to get clearance. We were kept amused by children reacting to their reflection in the window panes.

In the cities when we stopped at the traffic light the beggars would knock on the windows and flower girls wave their bouquets for us to buy. We became a menace to some as our "Bug" was taught to obey traffic rules. If no policeman was at the intersection the red light was not observed by many. Drivers used their horn (mostly air horns) so conversation was limited.

During one of Calvin's literature distribution trips to a congested part of the city the "Bug" saved his life. He and Anil, a Bengali teenager, headed down a narrow street moving slowly as they handed leaflets out the windows. Suddenly the crowd was growing and closing in on the car and stones began hitting the sides of the car. Quickly closing the windows Calvin immediately increased speed. Out of reach of the stone, instead of breathing a sigh of relief, they were struck by fear as the "dead end" barrier loomed ahead.

They would have to turn around and steer their wheels through that same crowd and more stones. Both of them praying, and the car cooperating, they accelerated as much as they dared and moved cautiously through the mass of faces. Stones and clods of dirt hit the car on all sides as people scattered clearing a path for their race to freedom. We escaped unharmed, but the car would always carry the scars, especially in the rear.

A short time later with dents still visible we visited the palace for a prearranged visit with a long time friend who now was the President of Bangladesh. Had the angry stone throwers known we were friends of the President, and had the President known his countrymen had mistreated us, both would have been embarrassed. As we approached the palace gate, the uniformed guards saluted us and the "Bug" (car).

One time its rear window and rear lights were stolen during daylight hours while it was parked in our driveway. We went to the nearest junk shop and bought them back. We dared not leave the car when we had it serviced or repaired for fear the good parts would be replaced by the inferior. Calvin's presence insured quick service as well. It was a great opportunity to meet new people and to distribute tracts.

For twenty-one years the "Bug" was our faithful companion and served well with the same engine and coat of paint. We salute the youth of the Pennsylvania-Delaware District for bringing the "Bug" and us together. We sold it for $1,000 when we retired from Bangladesh. The new owners have added 12 more years to it's life. Long live the Bug!

Chapter Thirty-Two

Eviction
*"Success is getting up one more time
than you fall down."*
–Anonymous

Sunday, January 5, 1969, is a date we shall long remember. We were renting a large one-story house with a long-term lease on one of the main thoroughfares in the capitol city. The spacious sitting room area became the meeting place for the now growing group of Christians. We lived in the remainder of the house. One day we received a written notice from the landlord's lawyer requesting us to vacate the house at once as the owners desired to live in it.

This meant breaking a lease. We learned later that the Muslim neighbors had complained about the Christians starting a church in their area. The lease agreement included the temporary use of part of the building for Christian Prayers.

In the meantime the owner was concerned that the Christian prayer service in the house would have the same implications as Muslim public prayer in any building. When any place is used for Muslim public prayers over a long period of time, that place, be it an empty lot, rented building or a tent, becomes a mosque and cannot be sold.

Cal felt it was "God's will" that we should stay. I felt we should start packing for moving. He prayed, I packed. However, we did start looking for another house.

At the close of a prayer meeting one night as we were leaving the building one of the men discovered his cycle had been stolen, even though it was locked. This was a great loss for there was no way he could replace it. Not knowing what to do and understanding it was another display of intolerance toward Christians, Calvin suggested we pray. While we were praying two boys came running shouting that the thief had been caught two blocks away, carrying a locked cycle. After delivering the thief to the police station, we returned to complete our prayer with thanksgiving. The police were amazed and considered it extremely unusual that the thief had been caught and that the cycle had been returned. We, however, were not surprised.

After two weeks we still had not found a building for residence that could be used as a meeting place. The owner hired University students who forced their way into our living quarters, threatened our lives and forced Calvin to sign a paper that we would vacate on a certain date. It was Christmas week. We asked for time to finish our celebration of New Year's Eve and we would vacate January 1. Reluctantly the landlady consented.

December 31, while the Christians were still singing a closing hymn, the doorbell rang and continued to ring. The angry students had returned and insisted we leave the building at once. After weeks of harassment and built up tensions the wear was beginning to show on us. I had lost 15 pounds. It was hot and we had spent many sleepless nights. So we decided to vacate at once even though it was dark and we had no place to go.

We sent two men out to look for an empty building which we could rent for storage. Someone else hired ten man-drawn carts on which we loaded our personal belongings and church furnishings including a small organ. The rest of the group took down the drapes, folded the chairs, collected song books, and helped to load the carts.

We found two rooms in a narrow lane two blocks away, in which to store everything. A missionary couple, Phil and Julie Parshall, invited us to come to their home until we could find a place to live. We lived with them five weeks, during which time we formed a bonding friendship that continues to this day.

The congregation, not missing a service, continued to meet in one of the two rooms we had rented for storage. Eventually we moved into one of those rooms. Shifting the drums and stacking furniture we were able to make room for a bed. I cooked on a one burner kerosene stove perched on the top of a metal drum while the search continued for a suitable location in that community.

Chapter Thirty-Three

New Location
"Every cloud doesn't mean a storm."
–Anonymous

One day we discovered "401 New Eskaton," just a block from the house from which we were evicted. It was almost in sight of the cramped quarters where we were living temporarily. We had passed that house often but since there was no "for rent" sign we ignored it. On this particular day we decided to at least inquire from the occupants.

It was a two family house, 100 yards off the main road down a private lane. We could live upstairs and the church could locate on the ground floor. It had a yard and garage and was surrounded by a seven foot brick wall. Ideal! However, it was occupied.

I felt impressed to knock on the door and inquire if the occupants planned to move soon. It was then I learned that the apartment upstairs was vacant and the ground floor would be available in a month. Securing the landlord's address and phone number, we set to work.

We located the owner who agreed on a long-term lease with permission to use one floor for Christian services. He even consented to our removing part of a partition to enlarge an area for worship services if we would replace the wall before vacating the premises.

It proved to be the turning point in our ministry. We lived on the second floor of that building for 21 years. We bought the neighboring lot and built the church center which is the largest Christian meeting place in the country. If we had not lived in that location we would not have bought that land.

It has always been a struggle to determine the will of God when the human element is involved. God knows that we honor Him, we seek His help, we need His wisdom and good judgment, yet He lets us make some very important decisions, apparently on our own. We can only believe unconsciously He has influenced our decisions.

Chapter Thirty-Four

Hospitality
"He who refreshes others will himself be refreshed."
–Proverbs 11:25

In the new church I taught Sunday school classes for children and Bible classes for women. I joined Calvin for home and hospital visitation and even traveled with him in village evangelism, but my greatest fulfillment came through the hospitality ministry. During those times I learned the "art of listening."

Our four room apartment included two bedrooms. One bedroom would be a guest room for missionaries who traveled to the capital city for shopping, business, to renew visas, and to experience a change from village life. They came from various religious backgrounds: from the States, New Zealand, Australia, England, Sweden, Norway, Denmark, Finland and Switzerland. They sat at our table, slept in our beds, read our books and prayed with us. As a result many of them experienced the baptism of the Holy Spirit. We built lasting friendships.

After the congregation moved to the new church building, Calvin used one room of the apartment on the ground floor as his office, another room as a prayer room, and the third room became a guest room for

Bengali pastors who often had reasons to travel to the capital city. In addition to providing this service we enjoyed great fellowship at meal times and Calvin had opportunity to mentor many.

From the very beginning we observed open house in our home on special holidays, feeding up to 150. We would include homemade American sweets and cake. People were very quick to observe every move we made, interpreted our attitudes, facial expressions, conversation and treatment of the underprivileged.

We came under criticism by some of our colleagues as we tried to live on a standard that would allow the local people to be comfortable in our home. It proved fruitful in every way. I never forgot the comment of one of the pastors who said, "We don't care how much money you have or how expensive a house you live in, if you gladly share your home and your time with us."

Marte Irene, a Norwegian missionary was a guest in our home for one week. On Saturday she bid farewell and proceeded to the train station for the trip north to a Girls School where she served. Imagine her surprise when she saw the train pull out of the station just as she arrived. Now what?

Within an hour we found Irene on our doorstep. She remained with us several more days. One morning she came to me as I was ironing clothes and asked, "How did you know that I was interested in the baptism of the Holy Spirit?" My reply of course was, "I did not know." We had purposely placed literature on the subject on the table in the sitting area. She had been reading a book and now was ready.

I called Calvin and we knelt to pray with Irene. Within moments her expression changed. She jumped to her feet and began to walk around with hands upraised speaking in her new prayer language. What a transformation! On her next trip to Dhaka she brought her friend Oluva, also a Norwegian missionary, who had a similar experience.

Chapter Thirty-Five

Early Believers
*"The Gospel is good news
only if it arrives in time."*
–Carl Henry

A Muslim businessman saw an advertisement in the newspaper about the Christians celebrating Easter, the resurrection of Jesus. He was taught that Jesus was a prophet and did unusual things while on earth but did not die on the cross nor was He resurrected from the dead. He believed Jesus was taken away to heaven by Allah and would return someday.

Curious, he made his way to the Bible Society with a list of unanswered questions. The officer in charge feared this man may decide to leave his former religion and become a Christian and the Bible Society could lose their registration with the government. They would then no longer be able to sell and distribute Bibles. They therefore referred him to Calvin.

Calvin answered his questions with Bible in hand as they sat together in a small private prayer room and then asked Him if he believed Jesus was who He said He was. The man said yes. As they prayed, the miracle of salvation happened and the man jumped to his feet with hands raised, his face beaming. He said something had happened inside him and he had peace at last. In an attitude of praise and thanksgiving the man began to speak in a language he did not understand and was filled "with great joy."

He turned to Calvin and asked, "Can Jesus heal my stomach ulcers?" Again they prayed and all pain left his stomach never to return. Three miracles had taken place: salvation from sin, Holy Spirit baptism, and physical healing. This seemed more than he could contain.

Immediately he began to tell others what had happened and the very next day brought four of his friends: a college principal, a businessman, and two engineers. He wanted Calvin to pray for them too. This man was a stranger one minute and a brother the next. He now knows the true meaning of Easter.

Mr. Huq, a Muslim in distress, was walking past the A.G. church one evening and decided to look inside. There he saw a group of men sitting in a circle, cross legged on mats. They appeared to be praying, some with hands raised, some with heads bowed and all with eyes closed. He entered and sat at a distance from them.

When Calvin opened his eyes he saw the stranger. Moving closer to him, Calvin asked why he had come. Mr. Huq told him of a car accident six months previously, that left him with a broken bone in his left arm. A doctor had set the bone incorrectly so now he could no longer raise his arm above his waist and he often experienced pain. He was taking an evening walk and had just decided to look inside the church. He had heard that Christians pray for healing.

After Calvin introduced him to Jesus through several scriptures the man's face lit up and he said, "I believe this Jesus can heal me." As Calvin prayed for him in the name of Jesus, Mr. Huq suddenly jumped to his feet raised his left arm and began waving it back and forth above his head. He was instantly healed.

He continued to attend prayer services and every time he saw us after that he raised the left arm in praise to God. Several years later we saw him in the parking lot of the church with his arm upraised giving testimony to someone.

The charismatic movement reached Bangladesh as well. Many Catholics were experiencing a new spiritual awakening and needed questions answered. Some nuns invited us to conduct a Bible study for them once a week on the Catholic school premises. We sang the same worship choruses as the Pentecostals, raised our hands, prayed simultaneously and spontaneously without the prayer beads or memorized prayers. It was refreshing, to say the least.

One afternoon two Catholic nuns and a Catholic father rang our doorbell. They had come to learn more about the Holy Spirit. Within twenty minutes the two nuns, one from Canada and one from Bangladesh, sitting side by side on a couch were praising the Lord in a new language. The Italian priest was so filled with this new Presence that two hours seemed like two minutes as he knelt on the hard cement floor. He had just experienced the "spiritual new birth." Though they continued to attend their traditional church, they kept contact with us and mentioned that they still prayed in their prayer language.

A Muslim friend, after numerous visits and prayer with Calvin, found great joy as He put his faith in Jesus. Looking at Calvin he said, "I believe." There was an outstanding transformation in his life.

As Calvin sat with him on one occasion talking about this new life the man became very serious and looking straight into Calvin's eyes, asked, "Did your father know about this message?" Calvin nodded yes. The man continued "Did your grandfather know?" Again Calvin nodded yes. This new disciple's next words are forever imprinted in our memory: "My father and grandfather died without hearing this message."

Chapter Thirty-Six

Miracles of Healing
*"Whatever it is that makes me
tick needs rewinding."*
–Anonymous

Mrs. Lyngdoh, a widow had been attending our services for several years. She had served as an army nurse in India for twenty years. Now she was dying in our car while we drove her to the tuberculosis hospital. A half hour earlier her handicapped daughter had come running to our house with the news that her mother was bleeding. We found her in her home unconscious after spitting up more than a quart of blood.

As Calvin drove the five miles through the congested traffic of the capital city, the daughter and I sat in the back seat with Mrs. Lyngdoh lying across our laps. When we heard the death rattle and noticed her breathing had ceased, Calvin began to rebuke death in the name of Jesus and continued doing so until we reached the hospital.

We had phoned ahead to ask the medical staff to prepare a bed for a patient which we would deliver by car. Their immediate reply was, "no vacancy." Calvin insisted that the patient would die without immediate help. Still they refused. Even though we suggested they put a bed in the hallway as they often did for extra space, they still declined. We proceeded to tell them we were bringing the patient regardless.

Mrs. Lyngdoh revived slightly as we lifted her from the car. Observing her the doctor said she was too far gone to save and told the nurses not to give her the expensive imported medicine. After she was placed on a bed and a nurse assigned to her care we returned home.

The next day when we went to see her she was sitting up in bed taking nourishment. We learned from the nurse that the doctor had decided to treat her when she revived. In a week's time she was discharged. Again prayer in the name of Jesus had restored life and health. She lived seven more years.

The call came early in the morning. Irma, one of our Christians was dying by choking. This had continued throughout the night and at this point she had to be held down in bed. Earlier she had run out into the dark night waving her arms and making a choking sound. We knew this had to be a manifestation of evil power that controlled her.

After questioning the father we learned sixteen year old Irma had been given a piece of candy the day before. Not long after that the choking began. It is not uncommon in that area for people to place curses on people through food. We could see the young woman was turning blue and unless delivered would soon die.

What would Jesus do? This was always utmost in our minds when we faced such situations. So in the name of Jesus we commanded the demon to release his influence on her. By now she was screaming and coughing. We continued to pray. It happened! She suddenly sat up with these words, "It is gone. I am free." Irma continued to improve and gave public testimony in the church.

Mr. Hossain, a Muslim, had an inoperable brain tumor and the family was waiting for him to die. He lived in our neighborhood and had heard that Christians pray for the sick. Calvin and I were invited to the home for prayer. Sitting beside the dying man was his teenage son who had said (we found out later) that if his father is healed when the missionary prays, he would believe in Jesus.

Having fasted and prayed before coming Calvin knelt beside the board bed where the man lay motionless. Reaching out his hand he began to ask God to heal his friend in the name of Jesus. Within minutes a change took place. Mr. Hossain opened his eyes and began to talk. He was instantly healed, sat up in bed, then stood to his feet.

The whole family began to attend church services and 30 years later the teenage son is still actively serving the Lord in one of the largest Assembly of God churches in Bangladesh. The last time we met him in 1999 he reminded us of the incident and how he kept his promise to serve the Lord if his father was healed.

Chapter Thirty-Seven

God's Strategy
*"After all is said and done
more is said than done."*
–Anonymous

Three hundred Muslims crowded on board the launch built for 100 passengers. Looking over the mass of people sitting in small groups on every available space on the deck, Calvin was suddenly moved with feelings of compassion and desperation. How could he reach this many people with the salvation message without causing a riot.

Then the thought came to him, prompted by the Lord of course, that the Bengali people read out loud. Even the children in the classroom and in their homes in the evenings read their lessons out loud. Reaching into his briefcase Calvin pulled out a gospel tract and began to read. He was interrupted by a man sitting nearby wanting to know how come he could read Bengali. Then he asked for the little booklet and began to read it out loud to the group gathered around him.

Calvin reached for another tract. Soon that too was taken from him till the supply was exhausted and small groups all over the boat were listening to someone read aloud. In the crowd were some religious priests who had been watching the whole incident and finally approached Calvin in anger.

They asked if he had permission from the government to distribute religious literature. Calvin replied that he was not distributing but people were taking copies out of his hand. There was nothing more the accusers could say. God's strategy cannot be beaten!

On another occasion when we needed to renew our residential permit Calvin went to the government office with his application. He was asked to wait, as usual, in a nearby chair. Praying quietly he asked God for patience and wisdom. He felt impressed to do what he had done on the river launch – read a tract out loud.

Soon every typewriter in the office ceased and several pairs of eyes and ears concentrated on Calvin. Amazed that he could read their language they asked for a copy of the tract. Just as they were all reading their copies out loud the senior officer walked in. "What's going on here?" he demanded. Then he saw Calvin and asked, "Sir, what are you reading? May I have one?"

Finally, mission not completed, Calvin was asked to come back the next day. This was normal procedure. Again, the following day, sitting in the waiting room he began to read a tract, this time a different one. Again the typewriters stopped and each man wanted a tract.

In time the senior officer appeared and exclaimed, "Oh, it is you again! My wife read your tract many times and she requested that if ever I saw you again, to get

more literature. Is this the same one or a different one?"
Then turning to the man behind the desk, the officer
said, "I trust you are helping Mr. Olson." Calvin walked
out that day with the residential permit.

Some weeks later that senior officer arrived at our
door. Thinking we were in trouble we breathed a quick
prayer and invited him in. After serving him hot tea and
homemade cookies he began to talk. He asked
questions about the literature Calvin had given him
weeks earlier. His heart had been touched and he
wanted to know more about Jesus. We lost contact with
him after that. We can only pray that someone else was
able to help him further on his spiritual journey

When Calvin was Chairman of the Missionary
Fellowship he often had to represent the group to the
government. Daniel, son of Ken and Joan Litzenberg,
was due to leave the country the next day to return to
boarding school. He had just discovered his travel
permit had expired.

Standing in front of the desk of the man at the visa
office Calvin made his request for a renewal of the
permit. As happened so often he was told to come back
tomorrow. Tomorrow would be too late. Still he was
refused. Instead of leaving the office Calvin sat in the
nearest vacant chair. After ten minutes he returned to
again make his request. The officer became angry and
yelled at him. Calvin then left the office and walked
outside to the parking lot where he paced back and
forth for half an hour praying in his prayer language.

He returned to the waiting room just as a senior officer arrived who knew Calvin. They exchanged greetings. Then the officer asked so all could hear, "Is this officer treating you OK?" to which Calvin replied, "Yes." He walked out with the necessary travel permit. God uses unusual means to bring answers to our prayers.

Chapter Thirty-Eight

Poverty
"Just because God can do anything
He doesn't do everything."
–Anonymous

The dining room in our Dhaka city apartment looked out on the neighborhood garbage heap. I watched mothers and children rummage through the pile looking for plastic bags and any edible food while the crows and dogs awaited their turn. It was difficult to sit at our table eating a nourishing meal with that kind of view from the window. Eventually we moved our table to a porch on the other side of the building. This, however, did not eradicate the fact that we were surrounded by hunger.

One day I saw a small boy wearing only a loin cloth sitting on a pile of moldy bricks eating roti, a common flat bread made of whole wheat, salt and water. The crows encircled him after he made the mistake of offering one crow a piece of his bread.

One cannot escape the scenes of hunger no matter where you live in Bangladesh as beggars travel to every neighborhood. Often people steal to satisfy hunger. It is a constant strain to try to separate the genuine from the professional beggar.

One day a young girl about 18 years old knocked at my door. She was healthy looking and dressed like a low middle class person. She thrust a baby's bottle into my hand and said she needed milk for her infant son. The baby had been left at the railway station with a relative, about two miles away. She had been robbed while waiting for a train and did not have money for another ticket. Her story seemed authentic and it struck a sympathetic nerve. I gave her a minimal amount and helped her to pin it to her inner garment. I also filled the bottle with milk.

A few days later my neighbor described the exact incident. We soon learned of others in the neighborhood who had been fooled as well. We have so much and they have so little that it is better to err in giving to the wrong person occasionally than not to give at all. Part of the Muslim creed is to give to the poor. Giving alms gains merit so everyone gives something from time to time. This can be good or bad. One learns to share but it also encourages begging.

When we would stop at a traffic light in our Volkswagen "bug" we would be surrounded by beggars, mostly children. If we saw a "legitimate" beggar we would whisper in the Bengali language, "Wait until our car starts to move and we will give you something." If they all thought they would receive something we would not be able to move the car. Yes, we gave. Everyone gives, but poverty remains. Even Jesus said, "The poor you have with you always."

About halfway through our career I can remember being so overwhelmed and frustrated by the surrounding poverty and disease that I became depressed. I prayed desperately for help. The Lord impressed me I was not responsible for the 130 million poor people in Bangladesh but only for those who came to me for help.He, God, would control that flow. And He did. From then on we would give food or medicine. If they refused both, we knew they were not genuine.

We kept a barrel of rice in the entrance way to our home and everyone who came to us hungry received rice. For those who had no way of cooking the rice, we would arrange for a free hot meal at the closest sidewalk cafe. another alternative was to serve bread, fruit, and tea from our kitchen. I might add that a couple of friends in the states saw to it that the rice barrel was never empty.

Chapter Thirty-Nine

Rickshaws
"If you don't know where you are going,
then you don't know when you get there."
–Anonymous

T he three-wheeled cycle known as a cycle rickshaw is pedaled by one man for 8 to 10 hours daily. His trips take him up and down hills and over gravel, dirt or tarred roads with potholes. It is the most popular means of transportation and the number of them in the city in 1990 was well over 100,000.

Rickshaws are privately owned and anyone is permitted to own one or even a fleet of rickshaws provided he has money and can obtain a permit to operate each one. Each rickshaw must be registered in the municipality and there is a limit to the number of permits that are issued. Many are unregistered and in some cases several registered under the same number.

A new rickshaw could be purchased for $300 in 1990. The owner then must find an experienced and reputable rickshaw driver. No owner drives his own rickshaw. He may sell his rickshaw and registration permit anytime.

The driver takes the rickshaw at 6 a.m. and works until perhaps midnight, and can keep all money above what he has promised the owner as a rental fee. Any major repair is paid by the owner. Since the rickshaw is a combination of tin and wood on an iron frame it is very vulnerable on the congested city streets with trucks, cars, and buses. The driver's livelihood depends on how skillfully he can wend his way through traffic without an accident.

Many die from collisions due to inexperienced drivers. Sometimes people fall off the cycles and are injured by other traffic. Clothing may get caught in the rear wheels of the cycle. One woman while disembarking had such a problem and was dragged several feet before the driver became aware. Fortunately the cycle was not moving very fast.

Only twice did I have a mishap while riding in one of them. I remember once jumping from a rickshaw as I saw a potential accident heading our way. Also I gave birth prematurely to our still born daughter after riding in a rickshaw that hit a pothole in the road.

It is not easy to embark or disembark from a rickshaw. One must step high to reach the seat and then jump down at one's destination. The seat is often plastic covered wood with no cushion or springs. I am sure that is how I developed a problem in the coccyx area, requiring treatment. There is nothing to grasp for support in times of sudden stops or bumps in the road. Often the seat is tilted forward which adds to the risk of being thrown into the driver who pedals in front of you.

There is a collapsible hood made of plastic stretched over a bamboo frame for protection from the sun or rain. However if you are taller than average you will choose to travel without the covering. There is no protection for the driver who continues pedaling in rain or sun. If there is a choice one tends to select a newer model, with seat tilting back and a roof high enough to sit under.

Many make their living at painting designs and scenes on the rickshaws which are colorfully decorated. After the War of Liberation war scenes were in vogue. Now you see romantic scenes and even some western cowboy pictures. Sometimes whole families of five or six will overflow the seat and sit on the footrest. The price is the same no matter the load.

One must bargain for the fare, often winning and sometimes losing. If other rickshaw drivers are vying for your service you win the bargain. Competition is high. Arriving at your destination you will be asked for a tip which would bring the total up to what he had originally asked for. If you refuse he might trail you down the road until you tip him.

Drivers do work hard and they deserve every coin they receive. One's emotions rise and sink as the driver winds his way through traffic perspiring until his clothes are soaked and the veins of his legs swell. Seeing the plight of the men who peddle makes me angry and sympathetic at the same time.

Many people prefer walking as it is cheaper, more convenient, and in some cases just as fast. It is not unusual for people to walk five miles a day to and from work.

Chapter Forty

Dilu Road
*"Acceptance: Making the best of it
when getting the worst of it."*
–Anonymous

G uests from America who were visiting us decided
to take a walk. They had not gone far when they
suddenly returned. They had seen a large gathering a
block away and interpreted it as a riot. It turned out to
be a group of people crowded around a TV located in
the front of a store on Dilu road. Crowds are always on
the streets of Dhaka, a city of ten million.

Dilu Road could hardly be called a road. It is the
width of one car, a lane that paralleled the lane to our
rented apartment, both leading off the main road. From
our dining room window we could look across an
empty lot to Dilu Road. Our lane was private but Dilu
Road was open ended. It developed many dead end
lanes on it's half mile winding journey.

A mosque with a two story high minaret gave the call
to prayer five times a day beginning at 5 a.m. Open
shops sold daily necessities. A barber shop, pharmacy,
bakery, and snack shops lined the road. The tailor who
made my clothing alterations had his 6 by 10 foot
cubicle tucked in between two other shops.

Shopkeepers sat cross-legged on the platform in their allotted space within reach of passersby. They could reach anything on the shelves without moving. The roadside cafe cook prepares food and makes a sale without changing position. At night he may sleep in his shop after dropping the shutter to protect himself and his shop.

At certain hours the road was full of pedestrians going to work, and three wheel rickshaws seeking a fare. Cars entering the lane at those times somehow managed to navigate, often to the physical discomfort of the pedestrians.

The pungent odor of spicy curried foods mixed with the even more powerful odors escaping from the area dump and the open drains seemed to penetrate every home including the bedding, clothes, and curtains. Bars on windows served as protection for those within and kept the uninvited out. A common sight is a child standing on the window sill holding on to the bars that separated him or her from the world outside.

I might add that mosquitoes thrived well in Dilu road and had free run of every home in the absence of window screening. Everyone slept under mosquito netting or completely covered their bodies with a sheet at night. Every night for thirty-five years we felt secure under our net tent.

Goats, dogs, and often even a cow occupy the courtyard of some dwellings while chickens run to and fro searching for food. Animals are not commonly kept as pets but run from house to house and dump to dump in search of food. If you want a good watchdog you feed him scraps of food and water drained from the cooked rice.

The lane was home to at least two thousand people

crowded into multi-storied apartments. Scattered throughout the neighborhood were two or three room houses with galvanized tin roofs. The rich and poor were neighbors.

One of the neighborhood dumps, seen clearly from my dining room window, bordered an empty lot where the children often played. I watched poor women and children chase away the crows and stray dogs while searching for plastic bags and eatables in the pile of rubbish.

One day I saw a truck drive onto that open lot. With an instrument resembling a pitchfork the executers stabbed the stray dogs that assembled at the dump and added them to the growing pile of animal corpses to be taken to a larger dump on the edge of the city.

This open area also served as the neighborhood courthouse. Any thief caught in the act would be brought to the large tree on the lot and beaten until he fainted. He would then be served hot tea to revive him and the procedure repeated. One day I saw them hang a man by his ankles from a tree branch and then beat him with many strokes. The thieves always survived and they continued to steal. It is a way of life for some.

As a woman I did not dare to venture far from home alone so I got acquainted with women of Dilu Road. Many Christians eventually moved to that area to be close to church, so Dilu Road became my turf. Mingled with other sounds one could hear the songs of Christians during a house meeting. Gospel songs on portable cassette players mingled with the blare of radios and television sets echoing throughout the area.

Often we were called on to arbitrate between two factions or to forgive those who stole from our fruit trees. Also we were invited to their weddings and funerals and quite often asked to offer a prayer. Many of these neighbors came to know Jesus and their lives were changed but Dilu Road remained the same.

Years later I would visit a family in Atlanta, Georgia, who had migrated from Dilu Road. They live as well as any middle class Americans, are employed by a well known airlines and are active in the church they regularly attend. Their first son died when struck down by a bicycle in Dilu Road but God blessed them with three more. Dilu Road does not change, but its people do.

Chapter Forty-One

Education
***"If you want to get what you've never had,
you must do what you have never done."***
–Anonymous

I wish I could adequately describe Dhaka University. The classrooms are tiny with about 50 girls on one side and 50 boys on the other side. The crowded wooden benches are arranged in front of termite infested tables. Names and slogans are engraved on the furniture by inattentive students through the years. Students sitting shoulder to shoulder and elbow to elbow frequently bump someone while they are writing. It is understandable how cheating on tests is so common.

The plastered walls are 10 to 12 feet high and look as if they could chip off and tumble to the floor at any minute. Black cobwebs swing from the ceiling. Birds fly in and out of the open screenless windows. Dusty fans are rotating from the ceiling circulating the 100 degree hot air, transferring the perspiration odor from the boys to the girls.

Ten year old ragged edge posters still clinging to the walls have been marred by political slogans written in colored chalk. The same powdery chalk is used on the blackboard so wherever your body touches you collect a little powder.

During recess the girls huddle in small groups with heads covered by scarves while the boys are at a distance in their own groups. Some girls are completely robed with small net covered slits just large enough to see through when they travel to the university. This outer robe is removed during class time.

Electricity is not dependable. Often the classroom is dark, computers stop working and of course the fans stop blowing air. Everyone perspires and since deodorant is not a cheap commodity and seldom available, you can guess the results.

The nicest toilet on campus is a separate building wired for electricity, but the bulb has been stolen. Once the door is shut it is pitch black. The commode is sunken even with the floor and one straddles and squats. This, however, is only difficult for the Westerner.

Students from countries in Asia, Middle East and Africa attend Dhaka University. In spite of the poor facilities many of these students go on for graduate studies in the U.K. and U.S.A. and are very competitive. The economy does not provide for maintenance or renovations so they are forced to exercise flexibility. How comfortable do we have to be to study?

Chapter Forty-Two

Black Thursday
*"It isn't necessary to blow out the other person's
light to let your own light shine."*
–Anonymous

The radio blared on November 12, 1970: "TIDAL WAVE TAKES 1/2 MILLION IN ONE NIGHT." Clouds had been gathering all that day and the atmosphere was threatening. By evening the winds increased reaching 50 to 60 miles per hour and the radio announced that a depression in the bay of Bengal was developing into a cyclonic storm. It was difficult to sleep that night with howling wind and the sound of broken tree branches and objects flying through the air.

The devastation that greeted us at daybreak was more than we expected. Due to the force of the wind, tin sheeting from neighboring roofs were half buried in our yard. Most banana and papaya trees had been uprooted along with some 60 to 70 year old trees. The wind was so fierce that even pieces of straw were forced into the barks of the trees. We were safe in our apartment building which had a flat cement roof and sturdy walls of brick, plastered inside and out. Others did not fare so well.

From the radio we learned that a deadly killer

cyclone with winds up to 150 miles per hour struck the populous southern coast. A 30 foot tidal wave journeyed 35 miles inland and then back out to sea taking every house and living thing with it. Eventually the returning tide would cast the dead upon the shores.

In six horrible hours hundreds of thousands of people were plunged into eternity. Official sources have confirmed more than a half million died. Entire villages were swept away with hardly any trace that people once lived there. The heaviest casualties were among the children and old people. In some villages relief teams were told there was no need for children's clothing as no children survived. Children were swept out of the hands of helpless parents into the rushing waters.

For months survivors were haunted with the memory of that dreadful night when their loved ones and scant possessions were swept out to sea by a wall of water. Thirty million people were left homeless.

Relief planes and helicopters from the United States, Britain, and other countries rushed aid to the stricken area. Relief teams were overwhelmed with the death and destruction they saw. Thousands of bloated corpses of people and animals were entwined in the debris. Mothers clutching babies to their breasts laid where the receding waters had left them.

World Relief Commission of U.S.A. responded immediately with funds enabling our missionaries to join the relief teams. Calvin joined a team in rebuilding houses for those who had lost everything. With a sleeping bag and change of clothing he boarded a launch the next day with relief funds in hand and traveled 24 hours to the disaster site.

Finding favor with a Bengali Army Colonel he was

given a tent which he erected on the damp ground. Since he was pastor of an International Congregation in Dhaka he would return home each Saturday, have Sunday services, and then travel to the disaster site each Monday. This 48 hour round trip continued for one month.

After designing a simple one room house with mud floor, tin walls and roof, he purchased lumber and C.I. sheets. The survivors were responsible for building their own houses under supervision. The stench of inadequately buried, decaying bodies and the sound of mothers weeping and wailing at the loss of their children kept sleep from overtaking weary bodies.

Densely populated East Pakistan (Bangladesh) has suffered often from the ravages and caprices of nature. Floods, cyclones, and serious epidemics have taken a huge toll of lives but nothing, within memory, even remotely compares with the November 1970 disaster. Thursday, November 12, became known as "Black Thursday."

Chapter Forty-Three

A Nation Splits
*"A nation wrapped up in itself
makes a small package."*
–Anonymous

B efore the people could recover from the tragedy of the 1970 tidal wave the government was thrown into confusion. For more than a month a group of our people gathered each night to pray. At the end of that March evening, the prayer group's faces mirrored deep concern. They knew that their country, its two provinces separated by a thousand miles of Indian territory, as well as by deep cultural and linguistic differences, was at the brink of civil war.

The government seat which rules the two provinces (East and West) was situated in West Pakistan which was more developed. However, the population in the West was considerably less than in the Eastern Province. Pressure was put on East Pakistan to join the West in making Urdu the national language. Unwilling to surrender their rich language which was so interwoven with their culture, the people of the East Province rebelled.

In the meantime it was decided to have national elections for a Prime Minister. Each province chose their candidate and due to the larger population concentrated in the Eastern province, their candidate won the election. Sheik Mujibur Rahman's Awami Party had captured a clear majority in the National Assembly making him the new Prime Minister. Outgoing Prime Minister, Yahya Khan, of the Western Province was evidently not willing to accept the election verdict.

The disappointed people of the East wing responded with demonstrations and strikes that paralyzed the country. Within days, planes and ships carrying military, ammunition, and tanks were secretly on their way around the southern tip of India to the Eastern Province. The tidal wave tragedy was soon to be swallowed up by the greater tragedy of civil war.

Chapter Forty-Four

Civil War
"Force is all-conquering,
but its victories are short lived."
–Abraham Lincoln

March 25, 1971, 11:30 at night, citizens of Dhaka were awakened by the sound of flimsy road blocks being pulled into position. Then automatic gun fire erupted throughout the city. In a matter of minutes parts of the city were ablaze as tanks and armored vehicles roared past our house. The West Pakistani army, with guns blazing, descended on the unsuspecting city. Later we learned that the newly elected Prime Minister had been kidnapped and imprisoned in the West.

Anything seen moving was under attack. Bodies soon littered the streets. We took refuge on the floor as a bullet came through a window, lodging in a book case. Among thousands killed that night was an Italian priest walking on His second floor balcony. The tanks reached the police barracks a mile from our home and in a surprise attack, leveled the buildings and killed everyone inside. It was panic! No one dared to show their face even to accommodate the dying and the dead. By radio they announced a curfew for two days.

On the third day two hours were given for people to secure food which became a nightmare as traffic clogged the roads and pedestrians jumped from stalled car to car attempting to escape the city. Those stranded outside the city and others hiding in culverts tried to reach their own homes before the next curfew.

Within days the local military was disarmed and the youth responded in retaliation with guerrilla warfare. The war ravaged the nation. Doctors, writers, scientists, and teachers were massacred. Officials estimate the war dead reached one million. Whole villages had disappeared.

At the close of the war many returning refugees could not find the location of their villages. From the piles of unsorted mail at the Post Office we received hundreds of letters we had sent out with Bible Correspondence Courses. They had been returned with these words, "Addressee missing."

On the third day, having taken control of the city, the military from the West set the curfew for 6 p.m. to 6 a.m. The dead were left on the streets to terrorize the people. We saw mothers lying in pools of blood still clasping their dead children.

Making our way through the city in our small Volkswagen, we passed swollen decaying bodies lining the ditches and mounds of earth which later proved to be mass graves. In one house alone we counted 16 dead.

The air was filled with the odor of smoke and decaying bodies.

During the war law and order had broken down and homes were destroyed, women raped, and hundreds of thousands died. Three families came to live with us after their houses had been burned. One pastor carried his two year old son for days on his shoulder through the tall rice fields in waist deep water, hiding from the enemy.

Our colleagues in another city, Howard and Olive Hawkes, narrowly escaped when a torpedo from a military boat on the adjacent river tore through the kitchen of their home. Josephine Spina, a member of our team, drove her car out of the American Embassy compound just two minutes before a bomb hit that building.

Calvin felt impressed not to enter a certain government building one day. He decided to wait in a nearby restaurant talking to a friend. Within minutes he heard the explosion from a bomb thrown into the foyer of that very building he would have entered.

It was at this time that we received a call to help rescue a Hindu family who had occasionally attended our church services. Knowing they would be killed if we did not respond, Calvin drove to the area, quickly loaded the family in the back seat, disguising the men as women, and drove them to a safe shelter. That family survived the war and became Christians.

Chapter Forty-Five

Terrorists
"Courage is not the absence of fear,
it's the mastery of it."
–Anonymous

It was November 16, 1971, the eighth month of the civil war. Eight o'clock one evening, during curfew, our doorbell rang. Looking out of the window of our second floor apartment we saw three men. From our window we questioned them. They had come secretly for copies of the Gospel of Luke in their language. Calvin descended the stairs and unlocked the door to the book room allowing the men to enter.

While he reached to get the Gospels from a bookcase he saw the men coming closer to him and discovered two had daggers and one a machine gun which they put against his neck and chest.

They took his watch, wallet, and wedding ring and asked where he kept his money. Calvin said he kept money in the bank. He wanted to prevent them from going upstairs to our apartment and thus exposing me. Angered, they threatened to kill him.

Just then I came downstairs to see why Calvin was delayed and was met by a man with a dagger in the dark hallway. Instinctively I gave a muffled scream.

Calvin, thinking I had been stabbed, pulled away from the other two men and ran to my side. He assured me our lives would be spared if we obeyed the armed men.

The men then followed us upstairs to the bedroom where we unlocked the steel cabinet and gave them what cash we had. I asked them to let us have the emptied envelopes. We were holding cash for others and the names and amounts were written on the envelopes. We were responsible to return that money. They promptly dumped the cash in a cloth and left the envelopes. Later I discovered a large bill stuck inside one envelope. Again, with a boldness, not my own, I asked them to leave something for us to purchase food. Again they responded by throwing the equivalent of two dollars on the table.

They tied our hands behind our backs, gagged us and commanded us to lie on the bed. For fear of rape we shook our heads in a negative sign. We knew the next move could be fatal. Suddenly they became frustrated and warned us not to tell anyone or they would come back and finish us off. They cut the telephone cord, locked us in the bedroom and hurriedly left with arms full of loot.

A neighbor who saw the robbers come and go knew their visit wasn't friendly. Risking the dangers of the curfew he ran into our house and followed our muffled call for help. Surprised and relieved to find us alive, he freed us from our bonds.

At the close of the war, we received a letter from a friend in Bloomington, Minnesota, Sharon Hennessy. She had a vision of our danger and prayed on the phone with a prayer partner, Irvy Gilbertson, for 15 minutes at the very crucial time when the men could have raped and killed us. We were saved by prayer and immediate obedience. Timing was a vital factor.

Chapter Forty-Six

India Enters the War
"It is a natural human tendency
for yielders of power to guard their territory.
Some people accomplish more in a short time
but have little sensitivity to others' work levels."
—Anonymous

The war, now in it's ninth month, had spread to every village in the province leaving devastation in its path. Ten million Hindus had crossed the border into India and some were living in new, empty sewer pipes waiting to be installed. This influx of humanity added a burden to India's already over population. As a result India had to make a decision about the war. If they did nothing, West Pakistan would continue to give India problems on both borders. The people of the East could not, without outside help, drive back the enemy.

At 2 a.m on December 3, 1971, we were awakened by the sound of planes overhead. India had decided to enter the war. Recognizing the sound of bombers Calvin urged me, and others who were taking refuge in our home, to run to the inner bathroom.

We were having meetings every night in our church with a speaker from Jordan who also was staying in our home. He refused to leave his bed saying he lived with night bombings for so long in his own country that he was used to the sound. After a couple nights we too got used to it and remained in our beds.

A quarter mile from our home an orphanage was blown up. A bomb made a crater on the main street, two blocks away. The window panes of our house cracked and shrapnel fell on our roof and yard. Within a week India was able to quickly paralyze the Pakistan Air Force and control the city of Dhaka while their ground forces spread out into the rural areas. They took thousands of West Pakistan military into India as prisoners and called for surrender on December 15 at 5 p.m. The people huddled around their radios waiting for the last minute surrender of the enemy.

On December 16, 1971, the surrender was signed. East Pakistan broke away from the Western Province, becoming the independent state of Bangladesh, with a secular government. Today memories of this civil war have not faded. For Bangladesh it remains the War of Liberation, a source of intense national pride that it threw off the domination of West Pakistan. But the West finds the memories painful, bringing the very rationale for Pakistan's existence into question.

Chapter Forty-Seven

The Rescue
*"Empathize: Instead of putting others in
their place, put yourself in their place."*
–Anonymous

The night of the surrender a man climbed over our 7 foot wall and came screaming to our door. We recognized him as the husband of a woman who attended our church. He fell at Calvin's feet and with tears pleaded with him to rescue his family who were now in danger because the enemy had used the roof of their house to shoot at people. The family was hiding in a storeroom and would soon be killed as the cleanup guerrillas were going from door to door, killing and burning. Calvin looked at me and I shook my head "no." He refused but the pleading continued.

Then Calvin recalled the Bible verse describing Jesus' commitment, "He loved not his life unto death." He agreed to go. Since our car was in the garage he drove the one in the driveway belonging to a missionary who had evacuated earlier in the war. It was dark, no street lights, no living person in sight as Calvin drove through empty streets. He passed a burning bus and heard an occasional sound of gunfire. During the four mile drive he did not meet another vehicle nor see another person.

He urged everyone to hurry or he would have to leave without them as the sound of shooting was getting closer. An anxious half hour later the group appeared. Five of them crowded into the back seat of the Volkswagen (Bug) and Calvin prepared to drive off. Alas, the car would not start. He tried several times in vain. The house searchers, shooting and looting could now be seen in the distance. This car, different from his own, was automatic and could not be pushed. The only hope was prayer so Calvin knelt beside the car and cried out to God for help. Once more he turned the key and the car responded immediately.

The passengers were taken to the Red Cross hospital and treated for shock. Within hours their house was looted and burned. It was an anxious hour as I paced the floor of our apartment not knowing if Calvin would return alive. Among those rescued was the elderly mother. We visited her the next day at the hospital and as we prayed with her she placed her faith in Jesus. She died that night.

Chapter Forty-Eight

Rebuilding a Nation
*"The man who removes a mountain
begins by carrying away small stones."
–Chinese Proverb*

D ecember 16, 1971, the war was over. The country was liberated. Thirty million people were left homeless. East Pakistan died and a new country was born, known as Bangladesh, the country of the Bengali people. Victory was sweet and bitter. It was time to rebuild.

Their Prime Minister, Mujibur Rahman (known as Bangobandhu, friend of Bangladesh) was released from an enemy prison in West Pakistan only to return to a war torn country. Bridges connecting towns and villages had been blown up, roads destroyed, whole villages burned, and in the general chaos, people searched for missing relatives, some never to be found. Ten million Hindus who had taken refuge in India returned to find their villages destroyed.

Millions gathered in an open sports field to welcome their new leader. Phil Parshall and Calvin, climbing to the top of the platform and standing a few feet away from Mujib as he spoke to the masses, took a prized photo. We ladies stood on the roof of the nearby five star hotel to watch the processions bearing banners; "Bangladesh is born."

In the ensuing months hundreds of volunteers from around the world arrived to assist. Calvin found himself as "tour guide" and "interpreter" for agencies who wanted to visit refugee camps and hospitals. On two occasions Calvin was able to introduce directors of foreign relief organizations to the Prime Minister and President of the new-born country.

A special building was rented to house the young girls ages 13 to 15 who had been raped and impregnated by the enemy. It has been reported by Bangladesh authorities that thousands of teenage girls had been abused in this way. Even though their religion forbids abortion they did not want their race contaminated. Such victims of abuse would find it difficult to marry if they continued their pregnancy.

Within days we received a phone call from missionary Mark Buntain in Calcutta expressing his concern for those of us who had remained in the country throughout the struggle. The following day he flew 20 minutes by jet to be with us. Walking on the empty lot next to our apartment building he and Calvin stood for a moment with heads bowed and expressed their gratitude for survival and prayed for guidance for the future. Lifting his head Mark remarked, "Cal, why don't you buy this empty lot and and build a church?" Calvin replied, "We have been considering this for some time and your words are the confirmation we needed."

Chapter Forty-Nine

Guarding the Land
*"Let the things that happen
to you work for you."
Paraphrase of Romans 8:28*

I mmediately after the civil war ended we began to feel the winds of change. Under the previous government, Christians were restricted in many ways. After the war we were permitted to visit the hospital housing the wounded freedom fighters.

We went from bed to bed and listened to the stories of men left to face the future without arms and legs. There, hardened guerrilla fighters accepted copies of the Gospels and other literature. When they decided to have a party to celebrate, we were on the invitation list and proved to be the only white faces in attendance.

The state owned Bangladesh TV began to sign on each evening with readings from the Bible and the Hindu Vedas, as well as the Muslim Koran. Our pastor was paid by the government for his gospel program which aired each Sunday evening.

On that empty lot adjacent to our rented house lived a Muslim family serving as caretakers for the land owner. We heard that the husband was very ill with bleeding ulcers. In fact the doctors had given him up to die. He had not eaten or taken milk for a week.

He could hear the Christians praying in our house on the other side of the wall. As a last resort he called for us to come and pray for him. With concern that if the man were not healed the reputation of the church in the community would suffer, Calvin hesitated. On the other hand if he were healed, it could mean the beginning of a great opportunity in this city.

It was with some trepidation that he and another Christian visited the little dwelling. He saw the man, reduced to skin drawn over bones, lying on a board bed. His wife and five small children huddled in the corner waiting for husband and father to die.

After a time of prayer there seemed to be no relief or change. The men prayed on. Suddenly the power of God came upon Calvin and he was prompted to take the man by the hand and say, "In the name of Jesus get up." The dying man immediately responded, rose up, began to walk, and cried out with excitement, "I'm cured! I'm cured!"

To the utter amazement of all he was completely healed. Looking at his wife he said, "Woman, start cooking." The healed man ate the hot spicy curried food which minutes earlier would have killed him. He was able to return to work the very next day.

When his boss, who had bid final farewell to him a few days earlier, saw him he could only exclaim, "What has happened to you?" After he learned of the Christians' prayer he insisted on a meeting with Calvin. It was then we discovered our healed Muslim friend and neighbor was the personal driver for our landlord who had now become the President of Bangladesh.

We drove our VW, with dents from being stoned earlier in the market place, up to the palace gates. The smartly uniformed guards escorted us to the palace where we were welcomed by the dignified and gracious leader. This was the beginning of our friendship with this outstanding intellectual and his family. There were frequent invitations to dine with them. We were also included on the invitation list for state functions.

The man God healed was guarding the land we coveted for a church.

Chapter Fifty

Purchasing Land
*"We must always add His resources
to our own when making our calculations."*
–F. B. Meyer

The rented house was soon inadequate for the growing congregation. We needed to purchase land and start building. One day we learned that the empty lot seen from our apartment was owned by the President. This was a valuable piece of property in the heart of the city on one of the important city thoroughfares. It was rumored that some company was negotiating to lease the land to use as parking space for trucks.

At 10 p.m one night Calvin called the President on his private phone and requested first option to buy the land on which to build a church. We were given that option. Now we had land but no money to purchase it. Under divine discipline we could not request funds or write letters regarding a building project. This project was to operate on faith. Calvin pursued the only remaining and reliable source, prayer. If we would trust God, He would bring in the funds, on time, from many countries of the world

Bob Pierce, founder of World Vision, and now Director of "Samaritan's Purse" came to Dhaka and contacted Calvin regarding some rehabilitation projects. As we sat at the lunch table he looked out the window at the empty lot and said, "Calvin why don't you buy that land for a church?" When Calvin replied that he was negotiating for it, Bob reached for his checkbook and said, "I want to be the first to contribute to it's purchase." He gave "$7,000 which became the earnest money for the 43 thousand dollar price tag.

The seven year old son of an American couple serving in a Rehabilitation program in Bangladesh who attended our church handed me an envelope one day. It contained twenty American dollars received from the sale of his toys. The local church contributed a large amount from their building fund. Still, more than half of the purchase price was yet to be realized. We had just twenty four hours before the deed would be signed.

As we sat at the supper table rehearsing the need for funds we heard someone call from the locked gate. It was a man from the Telegraph Office delivering a telegram. Our mission board in the States had sent word that the remaining purchase money had been credited to our personal account in an American bank and we could write out a check in Bangladesh. The following day the deed was signed in the Presidential palace on time.

The civil war had taken its toll on our health. Land had been purchased for a permanent church building. The building project would take two or three years. It was time for us to return to America for a long over due furlough.

After a fruitful time of ministry and enjoyable visits with friends and relatives we made plans to return to Dhaka. Facing us was the enormous responsibility of building a permanent residence for the growing congregation.

Chapter Fifty-One

The Impossible
*"When you come up against a wall,
can't go farther, can't move the wall,
can't walk through it; then lean on it."*
–Raymond Edman

Soon after we returned to Dhaka from home leave, we received a phone call from the President who sold us the land. He informed us that while we were out of the country the new government had passed a law which made it illegal to sell property in the capital city of Dhaka. There was a retroactive clause that made our purchase invalid. The President would refund our money.

Placing the phone on its cradle Calvin sat stunned for sometime. He was confused, disappointed, and frustrated. We had felt peace about every move to this point. We did not believe God was in this change so we went to prayer. For several days Calvin fasted and spent many hours in prayer.

One day the phone rang and a voice asked for Rev. Olson. I had become acquainted with that voice and I wondered why he should call. I could tell by Calvin's expressions and exclamations that the news must be good. The new law for selling land still held but the retroactive clause had been eliminated so we could keep the land and proceed to build. Again we experienced God's intervention.

The next move was to secure a building permit from the government which could take up to six months. Earlier we had asked permission to build a wall around the property to keep out squatters. At that time the official had told us we would have to get the neighbors permission to build a church in that neighborhood. This we did not do. To get permission to erect a church building in a Muslim country could cause further delay and even rejection.

Calvin filled out the necessary forms and prepared to go to the government office. He got no further than our front door when he felt impressed not to go that day. This was repeated each day for a whole month.

Soon he came under criticism by colleagues and church board members. Perhaps someone else should be responsible for the building project. After thirty days Calvin said, and I quote, "I got the green light, picked up my briefcase and headed for the government office."

It was the end of the working day and sitting in the waiting room Calvin watched as one by one the clerks left. Finally a man stood in the door and asked why Calvin had come. Presenting his application Calvin waited. There was silence then the official spoke, "Please come back tomorrow morning." We were made to understand that the usual procedure would be a piece of paper that says your application is being processed and the long waiting period would begin.

The next morning Calvin was again in that office and met the same gentleman. The gentleman handed Calvin a piece of paper on which was written, "Your permission to build is hereby granted." It contained the official government seal. It was unheard of that a building permit for any structure could be obtained in 24 hours. And no word was mentioned about getting the neighbors permission to build a church.

When Mr. President heard that the permit had been granted he remarked, "Not even I could get a permit that fast."

Rebuilding the country called for massive amounts of cement and the country's supply was soon exhausted. One needed a permit to import this important commodity. We could not build a church without it. Having fasted and prayed for the right time and the right man to contact, Calvin proceeded to apply for a permit to import cement from Thailand.

Upon arrival at the government office he learned that the commerce officer had gone abroad. Someone would take his place. So he waited in an outer room. It was Ramadan, the Muslims' month of fasting. At a certain time all work was laid aside and there was a mad rush to the refreshment stands or home to break the fast with light refreshment (Iftar).

The replacement officer rushing toward the door suddenly stopped when he saw Calvin. After a greeting he called for his secretary and ordered him to write a permit on government authorized paper and give it to Calvin before leaving the office. The impossible had happened again.

Within days we left on a two hour flight to Bangkok where we ordered the amount of cement to complete the entire building. Calvin personally saw it loaded on a ship. It arrived at the docks near Dhaka two weeks later and was transported to the storage room we had prepared. Armed guards were on each truckload to prevent stealing.

Now we were ready to build.

Chapter Fifty-Two

Interventions
"You can see a large field
through a hole in the fence."
–Anonymous

Calvin began the erection of a large church building without any training or previous experience. During the building project the Holy Spirit would awaken him each morning at 4 a.m. without an alarm clock, even though he had often been up until midnight working on the daily accounts. His 4 to 6 a.m. prayer time was very important as it was then he was given instructions. He would leaf through page after page of the building plans as he prayed. At such times flaws in the building were revealed and corrections were made that very day.

The contractors had bid low on the project hoping to make their money on less or inferior material. Knowing Calvin was not an engineer they would use smaller rods for pillars, omit the braces for the rods, dilute the cement, use smaller baskets for measurements and try to "take home" cement. They were utterly amazed by the many times their cleverness was overturned. They had not counted on intervention by God.

During the building process while the workmen were pouring the cement roof over the church sanctuary on a bright sunny day, the sky suddenly became dark and a strong wind developed. This was the month for the freak northwestern storms that usually came in the later afternoon. This was mid morning.

Since rain would spoil the freshly cemented roof and the bags of cement piled outside, the contractor yelled for the cement mixer to be shut down. Calvin yelled for it to keep going as he raised his hands and paced back and forth on the roof.

Watching from the verandah of our apartment next door I joined in prayer for divine intervention. The wind swept rain approached the building, split and went around it. It rained on all four sides of the new structure but not a drop on the roof or bags of cement.

So severe was the storm that a launch with 300 people capsized in the river 5 miles away and many were drowned. The contractor remarked, "God must be interested in this Christian Church." People still remember 30 years later how God formed a bubble around the church that day protecting it from the wind and rain.

Chapter Fifty-Three

Financing the Project
"Never doubt in the dark
what God has spoken in the light."
–Anonymous

From the very beginning God let us know that we could not raise funds nor ask anyone for help in building the new church. In a general newsletter Calvin wrote that the post war price of building material had risen. He had to delete that sentence. God reminded us that if we would trust Him, He would bring in the funds, on time, from many countries of the world.

The plan called for a two story building to accommodate 500 people in the sanctuary with overflow up to 1000. It had rooms for Sunday school and offices for pastors, district officials, and Bible School. The task seemed enormous. We often had to remind God that He said "He would do it if we would trust." Trusting was not always easy.

———————

Calvin was chosen as one of the representatives from Bangladesh for the Billy Graham Congress on

Evangelism to be held in Lausanne, Switzerland, in July 1974. As a candidate his expenses would be paid. He hesitated at first since we were in a building program and funds were exhausted.

Recognizing our need for a much needed rest a friend supplied the airfare for me to accompany him as a non-delegate. I stayed in the home of former missionaries to India, David and Berti McKee, now pastoring a the Swiss Reformed Church in Lyss, Switzerland. David was the man who served as a middleman introducing Calvin to me at the conference in India years earlier.

On Sunday morning Pastor David introduced me as a visiting missionary from Bangladesh. A Methodist layman, Andre Wolf, who had been impressed for weeks to give money to Bangladesh had no idea how to proceed. That morning he was led to attend the Swiss Reform Church instead of his own church.

When he heard my name and the word Bangladesh he knew this was his opportunity. The following day when Calvin arrived from Lausanne, the Methodist man came to the parsonage. He presented Calvin with a bundle of francs equivalent to three thousand American dollars. God had kept His promise.

One day long into the building project, Calvin came into the house with a distressful look on his face. He needed $1,000 by the end of the day. The mail for the day had already arrived with no money. In this poor country who would give this enormous amount. Unless this deadline was met the builders threatened to call all their men off the job.

Calvin let me know he regretted he had ever agreed to take on such a project. He wished he had never been born and further he wished he were dead. Wow! This was not like Calvin.

Suddenly inspired, I told him to go out to the building site and walk through the jungle of bamboo scaffolding used as supports. He was not to ask God but thank Him for meeting this new challenge. I would drop all work and spend the time praying for a miracle.

He came back within 30 minutes with excitement in his voice. While he was out on the site a rickshaw stopped in front of the building. The wife of a Presbyterian doctor said she had been observing the progress on the church building and wanted to have a part in it. She passed Calvin an envelope and left. Hiding behind one of the brick walls Calvin opened the envelope expecting about $100. To his amazement there were three zeros after the one. God did it again.

The building was taking shape and a date was set for the dedication. Again we needed funds or the completion of the building would be delayed. We were to experience a new challenge to our faith. God asked Calvin what he personally had contributed to the building fund. Up until now we had not sacrificed anything for the project.

As always Calvin shared his feelings then announced that we were giving all of our savings, $10,000, for the building project. This amount, mostly inheritance money, had been laid aside for a down payment on a home some day. This little "nest egg" was a certain kind of security for me, a woman, so it was not easy to give an immediate positive response.

To loan this amount was one thing, but to give it outright was another. For some reason it always took me longer than Calvin to hear the voice of God and obey. It wasn't long, however, until I knew this was what God wanted from us. I confess it was not easy for we could not see into the future. When we retired from Bangladesh many years later, Calvin, the only surviving member of the family, inherited the family home fully furnished. That was no surprise to God.

Chapter Fifty-Four

Lost Records
"He climbs the highest who helps another up."
–Anonymous

T he contractor was stalling for more money. We were concerned that the building would not be completed in time for the dedication date when representatives from the United States Mission board would be present. Time was also running out for the contractors. They had failed to complete the work in the agreed time. This meant, according to the written contract they could be released. Two weeks beyond the deadline Calvin notified the men that the contract had expired. From now on Calvin would contract the work himself.

This, of course, was not acceptable to the contractor or his men and they threatened any workers we hired. A new challenge. Calvin asked them to present their final bill for payment. Little did they know we barely had enough money to keep the laborers going on a daily basis. For the next three months the contractor did not show up with his final bill. Dedication of the Church Center came and went and it was soon time for us to plan home leave. We estimated we would need $10,000 to clear the books and none of that was in hand.

Toward the end of the building project I suddenly developed physical problems. During a general examination the doctor discovered a large tumor in my abdomen which resulted in pan-hysterectomy surgery by missionary doctor Viggo Olsen in ABWE's jungle hospital. Recovery in 100 degree temperature without air conditioning was slow and I was not regaining my strength. This became a great concern to all.

About this time we received a phone call from Hong Kong. It was our friend, Bob Pierce, Founder of World Vision and now Director of Samaritan's Purse. He was on his way to Bangladesh. Calvin filled him in on the building project and my health. When he inquired about our needs, Calvin mentioned the need for dried fruit for me. He arrived within two days with a suitcase full of dried fruit. It really helped me and many others as well.

Sharing a meal with us in our home, Bob suddenly pushed back his chair and said, "Cal, I feel led to give you $3,000 for building expenses." Then he looked Calvin in the eyes and declared, "Both of you are stressed out. I am not leaving here until you buy your ticket for the States. Furthermore, I am giving you a personal check to stop in Salzburg, Austria, for 2 weeks rest before proceeding to the U.S.A." And he meant it.

Two Rescue Missions in California, with whom we had no contact, had inherited several thousands of dollars. For a reason, still unknown to us, they each decided to send $3,000 dollars to Calvin Olson for the Church building Project. This, along with Bob Pierce's gift reduced the needed balance to $1,000. In the next day's mail there was a check for that amount from our home church in Willmar, Minnesota. It was the balance in their missions account for the year.

With $10,000 in hand Calvin phoned the contractors the next day and asked why they had not submitted their bill." They confessed they had lost their measurements and could not make out the bill. To their utter amazement Calvin offered them his copy of the measurements.

Soon the contractor and his assistant arrived at the church office, their attitude completely changed. They sat in the new church library, each reading a copy of the Bible in their own language, while Calvin checked their figures and made final payment.

Not long after that we boarded the plane for home leave, via Austria.

Dhaka

"Missionary Go Home" – prior to 1971

The rich and poor live on the same block

Asian toilet
in city

Congested traffic
in Dhaka city

Olson's
21 year old
Volkswagen
surrounded
by children

Calvin views intellectuals murdered by enemy during 1971 war

Dhaka city during flood

Olson's apartment and empty lot on which church would be built

Carrying bricks
for church building

Carrying concrete in baskets

New church building and four story annex for Bible School

Inside church building

Day school
for 700 children

Children
in classroom

Calvin helping
serve rice meal
to pastors at
conference

PART FOUR
Cal's Wife

"She is not a big woman at all. she is of ordinary ability; has no unusual ability; has basic education; is not beautiful; is not eloquent in speech.

She is only big because of the One she represents."

–Anonymous

Chapter Fifty-Five

Adjustments
"Trusting Him to be to me all my nature requires."
–A. W. Tozer

This book would not be complete without an honest portrayal of the woman Calvin married. Nothing is so important as that which is eternal. All that pleases or grieves the flesh is but for a moment. We learned to be peacefully miserable in adverse circumstances. To be a disciple one must give up all rights to oneself: right to time, privacy, culture, comfort, security and resources. Some of these I shall try to relate without prejudice.

Time

Our value and use of time changed with the change of culture. In Southern Asia one waits for hours at bus or train terminals or in a queue at the post office or government offices. We have waited an hour for late guests to arrive for dinner at our house. We had to learn not to be on time when invited to meals in their homes. The first meal of the day may be at 10 a.m. and the next at midnight.

A church service may not start on time and could continue for three or four hours. Often I have spent the night sleeping on stacked up luggage at the train station, airport, or on a floating dock. An Indian gentleman said to the frustrated American who had just missed his train, "Don't worry, there will be another one tomorrow."

Calvin was a better "waiter" than I. I was not happy with the day if I could not account for something accomplished every hour. Delays, interruptions, and postponements I considered time wasters and this usually resulted in great frustration on my part. Calvin invariably accepted such changes in plans with peace of mind.

Privacy

All of us desire privacy at times. There were times when even this had to be surrendered. Doors are meant to open and close. In Bangladesh an open door says welcome and a closed door is a challenge. In order to insure privacy in our bedroom we had to put a lock on the inside and outside. We never left the house without locking the outside of our bedroom door. The door to our apartment was left unlocked during the day for workers to come and go. The bedroom became my prayer and meditation room. It was there I would escape from people. There my tears flowed freely and it was there and only there I could be truly "me."

Loneliness

Privacy is not loneliness. Isolation spells loneliness. My outside activity was limited in the Muslim world. Living in a three room apartment with bars on every window I was often bored and lonesome. I have been lonely in my own home and lonely in a crowd where no one else understood English.

The greatest loneliness was finding myself the only Christian within many miles while Calvin was on two week speaking tours. We humans need fellowship and as Christians our survival depends on communication with other Christians. Many times this was limited to just writing letters. My pen helped me to survive.

Chapter Fifty-Six

Germ Warfare
"Risks are faith in action."
–Anonymous

We constantly fought a war with the little creatures of the world: flies, ants, roaches, mice, rats, lizards, spiders, bedbugs, head lice, and mosquitoes. For some reason from early childhood I had considered all of them enemies. A sudden streak on the white plastered wall of the bedroom spelled, "red ant army." It was easy to kill the army but not the tenacity of their community. In a few days the streak reappeared. We were friendly to some spiders as their webs caught mosquitoes and flies. We also had compassion on small lizards as we enjoyed their chatter and watched them snap at flies and mosquitoes.

Keeping the little world out of our food was a daily chore. The flour must be de-bugged after you purchase it from the market and then had to be stored in a warm dry place. Often we would see rice and flour spread on mats on the ground in the sun where our neighbors were fighting the same battle. Yes, I have eaten many ants, but always dead ones. I have also eaten peanut butter and jelly sandwiches which the ants had feasted on earlier.

We had bedbugs on our sheets, black ants in our food, flying roaches colliding with us in the dark, mosquitoes caught in our ears, and lice in my head. Not once were we bitten by a snake, scorpion, or malarial mosquito, though there were many narrow escapes. I once discovered a dead scorpion on the bathroom floor. One of us had stepped on it in the dark.

Returning home after a visit to a distant neighbor we realized it was getting dark and we had neglected to bring a flashlight. Noticing we were leaving without a light our neighbor offered to lend us a lantern. The path was narrow. Calvin was walking ahead as usual swinging the smoking lantern forward and backward to give us both maximum light when suddenly he stopped and yelled "shamp." Walking closely behind, I bumped into him throwing both of us off balance. We waited until the snake disappeared into the bushes and then proceeded home. A neighbor's lantern could have saved our lives.

Sitting at his desk one morning Calvin saw something brush against his shoe. It was a snake. Fortunately it was small and I entered the room in time to see it dangling from a ruler.

One morning I awakened with a strange burning sensation on my neck.

During the night, finding an entrance through my net, a spider had "licked" me. This left two second degree burns, the size of two fingers, which took weeks to disappear.

Perhaps the most scary incident was that of a scorpion which came to a men's prayer meeting. As usual Calvin was sitting on the floor with the others. Suddenly the man next to him began to scream. Then they saw the scorpion as it slowly wandered away. After killing the offender they turned to the victim who by this time was in severe pain. Prayer was the only treatment at this point. Within minutes the man relaxed and exclaimed that the pain was gone. That scorpion had wandered between Calvin's and his friend's foot, a distance of four inches.

Perhaps the most serious experience was the time we went to Cox's Bazaar on of the Bay of Bengal where we had gone for a rest. The white sandy beach, surrounding foot hills, and sound of breakers, along with less people to disturb us, was soothing to the nerves.

The first day we just waded up to our waist in water. Suddenly we found ourselves being pulled under. We grabbed for each other's hands and holding tightly we aimed for the shore. We realized however, that the shore line became further and further away. We were caught in an undertow pulling us out to sea. There was no one in sight or anyone who could hear our shouts. We began to pray, knowing this was our only hope. Continuing to push toward the shore at different angles we managed to gain ground, but we were panting harder and harder as strength waned. I cannot tell you what happened from then on. I only know we made it to safety, exhausted. What a blessing we had each other and both of us knew how to pray.

One evening as we were wading in the water we ran into jellyfish and Calvin was stung. With no painkilling medicine, not even an aspirin, and no medicine shop nearby, it meant waiting it out. In bed for two days in constant pain, unable to eat or sleep, he depended wholly upon divine intervention. I have never felt so helpless while I watched my husband writhing in pain as every nerve of his body seemed affected. For some reason the beautiful beach and clear water was no longer attractive. He did recover with no serious side effects. We had great respect for jellyfish after that.

Much could be said also about the germs we can't see that somehow managed to get into our food and then into our stomachs. I washed my hands more often in that country than in the States.

Chapter Fifty-Seven

I Lost My Kitchen
"Blessed are the flexible for they shall not break."
–Anonymous

One of the most difficult surrenders was that of "Queen of the kitchen." In America I would not even turn my kitchen over to one I loved the most, my husband. In Asia my hands went up in surrender and also in horror many times when I watched my kitchen being taken over by someone else.

"Kitchen Help" was a cultural practice – both good and bad. Even the very poorest of families would often keep a boy or girl in their home to do menial tasks. They would receive food and clothing in return. I was expected to hire a cook. I should have been thankful to be relieved of difficult tasks like shopping in the open market where the butchered cows and goats hung by their hind feet. The narrow paths between the food stalls were strewn with non-saleable items like rotten fruit and vegetables, animal innards and fish scales.

The cook would bargain for each item, then add it to his burlap bag. Live chickens with bound feet would dangle from the top of his shopping bag. Now can't you visualize me doing that? Nor could I imagine myself beheading the chicken, skinning it and throwing it into scalding water. Back at the kitchen in 100 degree temperatures the real work began each day preparing a meal from scratch. All this cost us $30 a month. Now that is the good part.

Yes, I should have been content if it were not for the "other things."

I arrived on the scene too late to prevent the cook from chopping chicken bones and meat together. Fish and their bones were cooked with potatoes and spices in a spicy sauce. Both sides of the toast were buttered. Another time he dropped the plate of pancakes and was in the process of returning them to the plate when I walked in.

When the food was cooked over a wood stove, smoke penetrated the uncovered food. Often food was cooked many hours before meal time and had to be reheated or even served cold, which is acceptable in Bangladesh culture. Unless I continually supervised we would end up eating sick-looking, over-cooked vegetables, while the vitamin-filled liquid they were cooked in was thrown down the open drain to the roaches and rats.

Amy Carmichael said it so well: "Where He leads I'll follow. What He feeds I'll swallow." I have eaten many things that I could not believe originated in my kitchen. We only had to eat them once. However, when as a guest in a village home, one does not refuse fish heads, cold turtle cooked in mustard oil, duck eggs fried in spicy oil, sun-dried (rotten) fish, rancid butteroil served over cold rice, curdled goat milk, and tea strained through a black rag.

For 40 years we experienced a kind of "germ warfare." In spite of the many bouts with dysentery, today I am a healthy person. A survivor. To this day my favorite food is curried chicken and vegetables eaten with rice, but I like it hot right off the stove.

One day a new lady missionary walked into her kitchen to find the cook squatting on the floor with a curved knife held by his foot, cutting up meat and vegetables. Unable to speak the language, she used signs indicating he should not use the floor but the table to work in her kitchen. The next time she entered the kitchen she found him squatting on the kitchen table with the same curved knife, peeling vegetables.

While helping with the laundry, two washcloths and 3 handkerchiefs were folded together. Clothes were folded wrong side out and socks not mated. After ironing, the clothes were folded in such a way that more wrinkles appeared than before.

Rice water was often used as starch for clothing. Too much caused a peculiar unpleasant odor. These had to go back into the laundry tub. Reaching for a match to light the kerosene lamps one evening I discovered the box was full of neatly packed used matches.

We did not always have a washing machine, so clothes were picked up by a laundry man, taken to the banks of a river, washed and beaten on a slab of stone, dried on bushes, and returned to us in a tied up bundle carried on the back of a donkey. The clothes smelled like the donkey.

We eventually bought a hand operated James washer. I needed help in pushing the agitator back and forth. If I left the helper unsupervised, there would be missing buttons, broken zippers or sleeves wrapped around the rollers of the hand operated wringer.

Today I am enjoying being "Queen" of my kitchen once more, wiser for the experiences of improvising and flexibility.

Chapter Fifty-Eight

Order or Convenience
"We need so often in this life the balancing
of scales, the seeing how much in us wins,
and how much in us fails."
–Anonymous

As an organized person I was suddenly faced with a new challenge. It was depressing to visit a government office. Letters and receipts were filed by stacking them on a large nail. The office was shared with flies and mosquitoes who came and went through the always open windows. Piles of papers ready to topple over filled every available space on desks in public offices. Open shelves lined the walls with stacks of files held together with string. If shelves weren't available they were stacked on the floor, reaching up to the ceiling.

Ceiling fans squeaked for lack of oil while kerosene lamps smoked from parched wicks. Broken furniture was supported by bricks "borrowed" permanently from some contractor's pile nearby. Empty cardboard boxes, open at one end, served as files for papers. Piled bricks served as foot stools.

Several bricks arranged over a hole in the office courtyard became a stove for making the endless cups of tea. Stained tea cups rested on each desk ready for the next of frequent servings during the day. Eventually we too drank out of those cups.

Most village people in Bangladesh possess very little. Without a closet, chest of drawers, kitchen cupboards, book case, table and chairs, where did they store things? Most activity inside the one room house took place on the large plank bed which filled the room. The first chore in the morning was to air the bedding. Later it would be rolled and placed on the bed against the wall, clearing the area for living.

During daylight hours, if weather permitted, most living took place outside. Food was cooked over a hole in the ground. Laundry was washed in the river or canal and spread on bushes to dry. Cow dung patties were spread on the ground or plastered against the mud wall of the house or bark of trees to dry and be used later as fuel. The branches of a nearby tree and protruding bamboo rafters of the straw roof served as racks for hanging things. Cooking utensils were placed in any of the available crevices in the roof or walls.

If it works, don't discard it, even though damaged by chipping, staining, cracks, scratches etc. While visiting in a mountain area of Pakistan I once drank out of a cup that had been broken and riveted back in shape with brass. The cup did not leak.

I marveled at the many uses of coconut shells. An empty coconut shell broken in two pieces served efficiently for serving rice. The brown hairy coconut covering is used for scouring pans and cement floors, massaging the body, or for fuel when cooking. I tried it and it works. I smile today when I think of how much of the above became a part of my life. I learned to improvise from observation and need. If they could do it so could I.

Chapter Fifty-Nine

Emotional Strains
"Pressures are continuing opportunities
for others to observe my true character."
–Bill Gothard

Early on Calvin gave me this plaque which still has a prominent place in my home, "Blessed are the flexible for they shall not break." Before I married there was the shame of being single. After I married there was the shame of being childless as our only child had died at birth.

I had surgery seven times, three in India and four in Bangladesh. On three different occasions I cheated death: during child birth, during the cholera epidemic, and when attacked by armed robbers.

Separated by 10,000 miles I could not attend either of my parent's funerals. This caused me a great deal of self inflicted remorse.

I was often bored from lack of mental stimulation. The conversation of the local women was limited to food, children, and husbands. I recall many questions from the women. They wanted to know who arranged my marriage? I replied, "My husband chose me because he loved me." They thought that a bit strange.

Then they asked, "Do you make your own money?

Our government makes ours." They wanted to know if American woman could nurse their babies. They nurse their children for 4 years, sometimes one at each breast. And of course they wanted to know if white people could marry dark people. Sitting in the bedroom with the women I envied the men in the outer room talking about world events.

I experienced frustration also from lack of opportunities to use my special training. Then I remembered, God doesn't necessarily give us the jobs we are fit for but He fits us for the jobs He gives us.

Two things made me feel very insecure: heights and crowds. Calvin loved both. As a boy the bigger the tree, the greater the challenge. Once when we were on holiday in Swat, Pakistan, we were climbing to the top of a steep hill with the intentions of sliding down a snow covered area. Wanting to be a good sport I proceeded by grabbing the roots of trees and clinging to large rocks.

Half way to the summit I looked up and saw Calvin and others at the top starting to slide down on the snow. I froze until they reached the bottom. They yelled for me to turn around and come back the same way. I couldn't even turn around. No one offered to come to my rescue. Perhaps they couldn't. Eventually, scratched, dirty, and exhausted I joined the others. Strange, I never feel that way in a plane.

Crowds still bothered me. I disliked shopping and milling around among people. If I needed something I bought it and returned home. Calvin loved looking at everything in every store and buying nothing. I avoided fairs, shopping malls, parades, and preferred speaking to small groups, while Calvin got great inspiration from a large crowd. I love people but give me one at a time. Did God know this before he sent me to a small country with wall to wall people?

It all happened in one month. The church treasurer, who also served as worship leader, confessed to committing adultery; the pastor in another major city misappropriated church school funds; the district bookkeeper confiscated money and fled to a neighboring country; the general superintendent resigned and I became sick with hepatitis and depression.

It took many hours of counsel and prayer with the offenders before restoration was made. I had to take complete bed rest for weeks. Others with the same symptoms spent months in bed and several Baptist missionaries with the same diagnosis had to leave Bangladesh never to return.

Disappointment in people, in situations, and even in oneself are not easy to deal with. Living in an isolated area, ten thousand miles away from one's own country and family, to whom do you turn for help? Recognizing our inadequacies at such times we knew we had to depend upon the Lord. Therefore we claim no credit for victories.

Chapter Sixty

Cultural Conflicts
"There are lots of human failures
in the average of us all,
And lots of grave shortcomings
whether they be great or small."
–Anonymous

S omeone has said, "We export ourselves." How true! Calvin and I both worked hard to adapt to the culture in which we worked. Our incentive to learn the language was to get close to the people and learn from them by listening to them. Culture is learned best through a common language.

The words, "Ugly American," are often heard abroad simply because Americans take their culture with them overseas. There are times when my contribution to Bangladesh was far from pleasing to myself, much less to God. Were it possible I would erase such incidents from my diary and my memory.

A tailor's shop was located at the end of our lane. We had to pass it everyday. The window of the shop opened on to part of our lane. It was his habit to throw scraps of cloth out of the window onto the path, making a clutter that this American decided was intolerable. Even after sending several messages for him to collect his trash and throw it in the proper place, even presenting him with his first waste basket, the rain of cloth scraps continued.

One day I decided to pay him a visit. First of all he was a man, then he was a Muslim. I was a foreigner, a woman and unveiled. His ears were closed before I opened my mouth. I can't remember a thing I said but I do remember there was no verbal response, just a continual depositing of scraps of food and cloth on my path. This was an incident I wished had never happened. I can only hope my good deeds outweighed the bad in that neighborhood where nothing is a secret.

We had almost completed the building of the Church center. After a few finishing touches the clean up would begin. Looking out the window of our apartment next to the church one day, I saw the caretaker carrying away some bricks from a neat pile near the church.

Since Calvin was not at home I decided to do his duty. When I questioned the caretaker he said the Bengali pastor wanted the bricks. I informed him the bricks were to be used to complete steps to the church foyer. He dropped the bricks and turned toward the pastor's office and I returned home.

I knew I had "blown it" again. After Calvin returned home there was a knock at the door and the Bengali pastor arrived. He requested that I be present and the three of us sat in our sitting room. He let me know he was the pastor of this church and he could do as he desired with the building materials (bought with

American dollars). Even though Calvin supervised the building project and also served as pastor of the English congregation, it was made clear that he, the local pastor, was in charge.

Since Calvin sat in silence, defending neither me nor the pastor, the monologue continued. Finally the pastor rose to go. Calvin suggested we pray together. This diffused the situation somewhat. Again I remembered I was a woman, and a foreigner. Some lessons are learned at a great cost.

During our early pioneer years in Bangladesh national leadership was scarce so missionaries had to assume some of the leadership. We learned early on that it is important to work as a team. When one missionary family went on home leave someone had to carry on his responsibilities. That's how I became treasurer for a few years.

This meant keeping records, receiving and distributing funds received from abroad for work projects and support of national pastors. The odds were against me. A woman in charge of handling funds; paying male pastors' salaries each month; listening to men's complaints; explaining rules to men, etc. I hated it. I wanted to decline and later resign. There was no alternative.

As often as possible Calvin was present when I spoke to men or I would have him deal with inquiries. I didn't mind bookkeeping but talking to men in a male dominated society was a strain and pressure I did not need.

To this day I do not know how I operated from our village home eight hours from a bank, with limited postage at the post office, no telephone, and letters of inquiry that came written in Bengali which I could not read. They scribble Bengali like Americans scribble English. I had learned only the proper method. I don't think I smiled much during that time and Calvin had a different wife for the duration. I am not very proud of my performance.

Chapter Sixty-One

In Sickness
"Lord, quiet my mind. Steady my hurried pace.
Break the tensions of my nerves
with your soothing voice."
–Anonymous

T he ultimate test of commitment to a "call" is when your spouse is sick and the available medical help is inadequate. One is tempted to go home to the States for treatment. Like most Westerners living in a third world country we often had "soft stomachs," "jelly belly," cramps, nausea, all caused from lack of hygiene, uncovered food, undercooked meat or stale food. Homes, shops and restaurants were unscreened and windows were left wide open for circulation of air. This was an open invitation to flies.

Due to the lack of communication facilities in the village and slow transportation, Calvin, during one of his many tours, could have died and been buried before I received notice of his sickness. In the absence of embalming, bodies must be buried before sunset the same day. Where there is no telegraph service, runners are still used to deliver messages.

It was April 8, 1975. On the previous day we had traveled by two planes and a bus to reach the Baptist hospital on the edge of a jungle where I was scheduled the next day for pan-hysterectomy surgery and the removal of a large tumor. The news was not good. The doctor warned it could be cancerous.

Calvin and I stood on the balcony of a "zero" class motel at Cox's Bazaar, a beach resort one hour south of the hospital. We were speechless as we held each other and watched the waves beat on the shore. Far from family, friends, and colleagues we cherished those moments we had together, perhaps never to be repeated.

The next day Calvin prayed, then said goodbye to me as they wheeled me into surgery. He tells of how pale the missionary doctor, Viggo Olsen, looked as he accepted this awesome responsibility.

Returning to the guest house, provided by the hospital, Calvin was greatly surprised to find Phil Parshall a Baptist missionary and close friend. He had traveled the many miles from Dhaka to be with Calvin during this stressful time. Phil and Calvin had spent many times of prayer together in the past. Now in this time of crisis he came to extend his support.

In spite of 90 to 100 degree temperatures, without air conditioning and with limited nursing care, I came out of that experience cancer free to serve yet another 14 years in Bangladesh.

It was 1979. I was awakened in the night with such abdominal pain I could not sit, stand, lie down, or keep still. The only medical facility open at that hour was the

Cholera Research Laboratory manned by a couple of foreign doctors. Immediately they recognized it to be a gall bladder problem. They administered medication intravenously as I lay on the examining table, the only bed available.

For 24 hours I managed trips to the bathroom carrying the bag of fluid. It was eventually determined that surgery was necessary. This meant two planes and a bus trip to the mission hospital again.

No seats were available on the plane. Providentially two doctors from the hospital were booked on the plane. One surrendered his seat to me and the other became my private escort. Calvin joined me two days later. Again, part of me was buried in the hospital grounds.

Once we had to fly to Bangkok, two hours by plane, for treatment for a blood clot in my right leg. When we returned to Bangladesh it meant a weekly trip for three months to a local clinic for a blood test. After standing in line for a half hour each visit to the clinic, I was seated along with many others in a dusty, screenless room with wide open windows. I supplied the disposable needle, cotton swab, and Band-Aid. Each time, as I turned to leave they asked for the disposable needle. I always gave it to them. It was sharper and cleaner than the ones they used again and again without being sterilized.

I never became acclimated to the tropical heat. My body was always wet either from moisture from above or from my own perspiration. One could not get dry after a shower as the humidity was so heavy in the air one's body heat produced continual perspiration.

It took days to dry the laundry without the luxury of an electric clothes dryer and in some cases no electricity and no fans. Often we wore smelly clothes and used damp towels.

There were times when I wondered why God sent me to Southern Asia when my body could not tolerate the heat. Perhaps the greatest discomfort was the tropical sun. I had sunstroke twice the first two years of service in India. From then on I could not be exposed to sun rays more than a few minutes without getting a severe headache and nausea. My head was always wet, even when the rest of my body was dry. The umbrella, rain or shine, was my constant companion whenever I left the house.

This limited my outside activity. It was especially difficult when we had no electricity and no fans. Often when visiting homes with a room full of human heaters and little ventilation I felt overcome to the point of fainting. God knew this and He did not deliver me from it but gave me the endurance to live through it. Even to this day I dare not stand in the sun more than five minutes. I am forever grateful to God for creating trees to provide shade.

Chapter Sixty-Two

Furlough Adjustments
"God didn't tell me I had to come back.
He only told me to go."
–John Tucker

Returning to the States for furloughs called for many new adjustments. After 8 1/2 years I experienced my first furlough in the spring of 1959. Calvin and I had married in India just as I completed my first term of service. We then served together in Bangladesh to complete Calvin's term of four years before the first home leave.

During those nearly nine years America had experienced great changes. We returned to Minnesota to discover a supermarket for the first time. I saw endless shelves of food; carts full of junk food. I wept, as I was reminded that two-thirds of the world go to bed hungry every night. I still had vivid pictures of women and children searching for food in garbage heaps. I remember a dying woman clutching a loaf of bread I had given her, too weak to feed herself as her infant son lay beside her on the sidewalk.

Calvin was back to politely opening doors for me, and I started shaking hands with men. Friends taught us how to use the washer, dryer, and dishwasher. A complete stranger showed me how to use the foot pedal on a water fountain, and how to operate the lever on the soft ice cream machine. And soon I too was pushing a cart full of food up to the checkout counter at the super market.

One thing in particular really bothered me. Every where I went I saw "Self Storage" signs and then I saw units like garages which are marked "for storage only." Immediately I was reminded of the story Jesus told about a rich man in Luke 12:18, "I will build bigger barns where I will store 'my other goods.' Then I will say to myself, lucky man, you have all good things."

How could I reconcile the fact that many people in South Asia eat only if they earn that day and many go to bed hungry, while Americans have so much they must rent storage units for their "other goods." Adjusting to American culture was not easy.

After the Government of Bangladesh refused to renew our residential visa, we returned to the States in 1989. We had both celebrated our 65th birthdays. Calvin was sick with bronchitis as we arrived at the airport in Minneapolis. Our parents had died. We had no living children and no home.

Pastors Larry and Jo Mather met us at the Minneapolis airport, took us to their home for three weeks and nursed us back to health. In time they drove us to Willmar, Calvin's hometown, two hours west of Minneapolis. We had only suitcases, no place to live and no direction for the future. God provided through our friends, Bob and Edith Johnson, who took us into their home for 5 weeks until we could rent and furnish an apartment.

Calvin insisted on my learning to drive a car at 65. If I intended to write a book about our life in Bangladesh I knew I would have to learn how to operate word processing on the computer. This, on top of all other adjustments, was overwhelming. Calvin, as always, was my encourager. The computer and I were not compatible at first but we soon became friendly and together we produced this record of our memoirs.

Living in the U.S. meant another change in language and culture. I found myself doing unique things like: touching my husband in public, walking in front of him instead of behind, speaking to other men, uncovering my head, wearing slacks, eating pork, eating with fork and spoon, sitting in chairs, buying without bargaining, wearing shoes in church, sleeping without a mosquito net, leaving doors unlocked, driving on the wrong side of the street, and obeying ALL traffic rules.

We were not used to the extravagance we witnessed. The size of garbage cans, the wasted food in restaurants, and the free use of credit cards disturbed us. We couldn't forget the price of a new suit would buy 3,200 gospels. We couldn't forget the women and children looking for scraps of food in the garbage bins. We couldn't forget the swollen stomachs of children due to malnutrition.

Did I look confused? I must admit, however, that I did enjoy hot showers once more, also Christian radio and TV, supermarkets, controlled temperatures in our home, freedom of speech, free movement, and freedom to practice the religion of my choice.

We are grateful to all who helped us fulfill our call

with prayer and financial support and who made our reentry to the States as easy as possible. We would have never made it in either culture without their help.

Chapter Sixty-Three

We Are Different
"Diversities are the spice of life."
–Marian N. Olson

We were different, perhaps even peculiar to some. We were the product of the things that had happened to us and the places where we had been, admired by some and pitied by others. We began as ordinary people. What made us different? We had been where the conflict of evil is open and tense and where there is fight, not fashion.

We had seen firsthand poverty not prosperity. We watched whole families die of cholera and be buried in a common grave. We had seen thousands die without Christ during a cyclone and tidal wave. We had witnessed communal riots when whole villages were burned.

We remember running from bullets and hiding people in our home during the civil war. We remember visiting the limbless at a guerrilla hospital. We remember 13 year old girls at the abortion clinic following the war.

If we didn't seem to warm up so quickly or or if we seemed unapproachable, remember we had lived for 35 years under a radically different social system.

If we stumble at the English language it may be because we have spoken the Bengali language more years than English. We had changed more than we realized. My parents on my first furlough thought I spoke with a British accent. And I did. The people from the sub-continent inherited their English and school system from the British. English was a second language for the people I lived and worked with. They had an accent all their own and I quite naturally acquired that and rather enjoyed it. I learned to speak slowly and distinctly using limited vocabulary. Well, that does not go down well with Americans and often Calvin would have to remind me to speak faster. As for accent, that changes easily with the environment. I was soon speaking with a Minnesota Scandinavian flavor. I did have to increase my English vocabulary and learn to spell all over again. *Webster's* dictionary became a close friend.

If life seems more serious to us it is because we have lived under daily harassments from the government through phone tapping, bribery, and even being shadowed by the secret police.

We can never forget millions of unanswered prayers that are prayed five times a day in the mosques and temples throughout the country. We have struggled with the birth pangs of a new church planted in a new nation.

In the big cities where many villagers migrate looking for jobs, they often end up sleeping on the sidewalks. At night you can see them wrapped from head to foot in a sheet as protection from mosquitoes. The drains become toilets, and a public faucet becomes the bathhouse. Often they must beg for daily food until employment is found. Many children end up as professional beggars, with no chance of an education. One morning I found a woman lying at our gate, dead from hunger. I came too late!

Perhaps the greatest change was seen in the value we placed upon things. Life had been unencumbered and without clutter for 35 years. We needed little to survive and were satisfied with the basics. Our joy was in being with each other and doing what God asked us to do. Now that we were on furlough people wanted to be kind and give to the "poor" missionary. When we refused things we did not need the average person could not understand. We were richer than they thought or could imagine.

Chapter Sixty-Four

Where Are Your Children?
"Children's children are a crown to the aged."
–Proverbs 17:6

A princess was walking beside a river early in the morning watching the birds flit in and out of the bushes when suddenly she noticed an unusual and larger movement. It was a basket. She soon discovered it held what she wanted, what she needed and didn't have, even though she lived in a palace. It was a baby boy.

During the many years of residing in Bangladesh our house was always "open." Everyday people came to see us. The neighborhood ladies on their first visit opened my closet doors and drawers to explore the contents as they examined every corner of the three room foreign house made of brick walls, and cement floors. Many of their houses were one room with a mud floor, thatch or tin roof, and woven bamboo or tin walls. The endless question was, "Where are your children?" Do only two of you live in three rooms? Why doesn't your husband take another wife? Then her child will be yours too. I was soon to learn that the main reason for the existence of women was to bear children. If so, why am I here?

Childlessness was my wound that would never heal and in their culture it was considered a shame. Our only child died at birth and is buried in the Christian cemetery in Dhaka. I bore the shame of being an unmarried woman in that culture for five years when I served as a single missionary and then for thirty-five years as a barren wife. How could I reach them, sit where they sit, think what they think, and feel like they feel. What did we have in common? Certainly not children!

I loved to watch their children. You can see them sitting on a pile of bricks throwing crumbs to the crows or searching the neighborhood dump for recyclable plastic. I watched babies nursing at the breast while their mothers worked eight hours a day breaking stones or brick to be used as aggregate for concrete. I once saw a grandmother, bare from the waist up, sitting on the bank of a canal. Her withering breasts served as a pacifier for her grandson while his mother worked in the fields. Boys rode on their father's shoulder as they walked miles to the area's community market. The children danced in the rain as the hot season is broken by the monsoon. I observed them gathering cow dung and twigs for fuel. It was not uncommon to see 5 and 6 year old girls cooking the daily meal or caring for the latest sibling; always carried on the hip.

A child knows how to play in any country, in any circumstance. Stones become jacks and ball and are used for hop scotch. They are hit with a bamboo stick in a kind of ball game. Like a child anywhere in the world they enjoy make-believe and produce mud pies baked in broken clay vessels, over a hole in the ground with a make believe fire. The trees become their jungle gym and they can mount an eight foot brick wall with bare feet in seconds. Older boys wearing only a loincloth play soccer in the muddy fields during the rainy season. Covered with mud only their eyes are visible as they pass the ball around the field with knees, elbows and shoulders, but not with feet or hands.

Dogs and cats are not considered pets but serve as guards against thieves and rats. However, it is not uncommon to see a child hugging the family goat. I was amused to watch a child protect his cow from mosquitoes by draping a net over it as it lay on the mud floor of the lean-to shed. On the other hand, fun is grabbing a puppy by the tail and dragging him home. Fun is also trying to catch the ducks that eat the grain spread out on mats in the sun to dry. First you chase the ducks toward the grain, let them eat some, then coming from behind grab their wings, then holding them just above the grain, let them take a last beak full, then carry them back to the canal. Fun is also stealing peas from my garden. It is only wrong if you are caught. The fact is I never saw them do it. It was probably "night fun."

––––––––––––––––––––––––––––––

At an early age some children, left to face life on their own, soon learn how to cleverly steal and beg for survival. I have watched them dig through piles of garbage on the roadside looking for plastic bags to be recycled or palatable food to eat. At night they might cover themselves with a cloth as they curl up at the entrance to some shop to settle down to sleep. A public hydrant becomes their bathhouse and the drain their toilet. Some of them would disappear and end up in a brothel.

One day we visited the largest Banyon tree in the world, in Calcutta, India. It was 200 years old and 1,500 feet in circumference. There I met an 9 year old orphan girl with only a thumb on one hand. She actually smiled at me. Talking to her I learned of the train accident which took her fingers and her mother who died trying to save her. Unable to work she made her living by begging. She appeared intelligent and had a winsome personality. I gave her an orange which she immediately began to peel with her thumb. When I inquired if she worked she replied, "How can I? I have no hands." Just before saying goodbye I placed some coins in her hand, enough for her next meal.

For special holidays parents may paint their little girls like dolls with mascara, rouge, lipstick, frilly dresses, and headbands that look like little crowns. In Gopalganj where we made our home for six years I was walking in the shopping area on a special Muslim holiday, Eid. I was attracted to a small boy really "dressed up." He was strutting down the narrow path between two rows of small shops with hands on hips wearing spanking new shoes and a "G" string with bells around his waist. That's all.

Chapter Sixty-Five

God Gave Us Family
*"Take this baby and nurse him for me,
and I will pay you."*
Exodus 2:9

M y experience was perhaps not so romantic as
Pharaoh's daughter finding baby Moses but I did
find my children in a country not my own and in a
culture that became my own. Even though the adults
stole from me, called me "red monkey" and yelled
"missionary go home," the children called me aunty.

One day while visiting a neighbor in our village I sat
on a stool two inches above the ground, before the
outdoor stove, which was a hole in the ground. I fed the
fire with straw and cow dung cakes while she cooked
the daily meal. I spoke to her in her language. I sat like
she sits. I felt her loneliness. Her children became mine
as they sat in my lap, pulled at my hair and left the scent
of their mustard-oiled bodies on my clothes and hands.
At that time I did not know that one day I would place
one of her children in a common grave during a
cholera epidemic. One day this mother would be dying
from kidney failure and would hang on to life as we
nursed her hour after hour. This baby in my lap would
one day steal peas from my garden, would stand on

stacked bricks to peer into my windows, and would strip the flowering bushes and fruit trees. BUT he would come to Sunday School and eventually come to Jesus, and someday become a pastor.

I Nilu

Also in that Sunday School class was NILU an eight year-old-girl who would one day be the mother of seven, all of whom would serve the Lord. The oldest son would use his computer expertise in the ICI Bible Correspondence Program which, in the beginning, sent study books, followed by a Bible, to every school teacher in the country. Later he married a girl who also attended the Sunday School. They migrated to the States where he received his masters degree in computer science. Before he was even fluent in English he was hired by Delta Airlines and today is the top computer man for the company. They continue to serve the Lord and are active in church and community.

Rose, born into a Christian home in India, came to accept Jesus at the early age of nine. While in college she met a young Hindu student who through many contacts with Rose left Hinduism to become a Christian. They later married and became parents of a son and daughter. The busyness of life with a family and career left little time for church and God. Soon their faith became weak.

After the 1971 liberation war in Bangladesh they accepted the directorship of an American Relief-Rehabilitation Program and were stationed in Dhaka, Bangladesh. Their children by now were studying in college in the States.

It was at this point in their lives that we came to know them. They attended the Assemblies of God International church service of which Calvin was pastor. We knew their spiritual life was weak and we began to pray for them and with them over the next eight years. They invited us to their home for dinner many times, and we often entertained them in our home.

October 21, 1980, the phone rang in our apartment. It was Rose. Her husband was divorcing her. Broken-hearted she reached out for help. I asked her to come for lunch and we would pray together. She arrived at 10 a.m. in tears. Calvin joined us for prayer that lasted five hours as Rose once more surrendered her life to the Lord.

At first there was a struggle to forgive her husband. She had spent many sleepless nights crying. She knew this would be a barrier to peace with God and with herself. She tried to bargain with God but somehow she knew she must forgive before healing could take place. Four times we knelt to pray without complete surrender. Finally she knew she had to make a definite commitment to forgive her husband. When the surrender was complete and forgiveness became reality she suddenly began to speak in a language she had never learned. This continued for some time and then suddenly she felt a release in her spirit and she was free to forgive.

We had forgotten about food or work schedule. Her transformation was noticeable by all as she continued to develop a close relationship with the Lord. Later she joined her daughter, now married, in the States. We were able to keep in touch with her up to the present time. What a beautiful Christian! Added to her natural beauty is a new and greater beauty that comes from within. She has ministered to many women who suffered rejection through divorce as she had.

Chapter Sixty-Six

My Neighbor Judy
*"She calls her friends and neighbors together
and says, 'Rejoice withe me.' "*
–Luke 15:9

Judy's mother was a Jew and her father a Muslim. They were our neighbors. There were times when we could hear shouting, abusive language, and dishes crashing against the wall. Today Judy is a Christian. She tells her own story.

"When I accepted Jesus Christ as my personal Savior at age 16 my heart found peace, peace like I've never experienced before. I had tried everything to become successful in my job as a private secretary, even working overtime. As a result I had a nervous breakdown. To get over it I began taking sleeping pills and tranquilizers, but it still did not help. Every night was a nightmare for me and most of the time I could not concentrate on my work.

"I would check my horoscope daily and act accordingly. But that seemed to make things worse. I was always surrounded by fear. In an effort to overcome fear I decided to be more aggressive in building friendships. I started to attend the Go-Go shows and other dances which led me to the popular set. I would also go to the movies with my friends.

"As a teenager I had everything I needed and wondered why I should bother about the emptiness within me, but I was too tense and could hardly think straight. I loved pop music so I would lock myself in the living room with the record player on full blast. I still felt a dissatisfaction within me and tried to figure out what was missing.

"Even though Pastor Olson and his wife would sometimes make a call, give me some youth magazines and invite me to church, I never went. Again I received an invitation and this time the invitation said that they would have Christian folk songs. So I went.

"This was my first time in six years to enter a church. It was a three day meeting. To my surprise, I wanted to attend again the second day and on the third day of the meeting I came to know the One who could meet all my needs, the Man, Jesus Christ. Ever since then I have been living for the Lord. I am no longer fearful but have peace. My future is in God's hands.

"There is no need for me to take any more tranquilizers or sleeping pills and I am no more what the doctor suspected me to be - a neurotic. My work now is so pleasant and I am able to take two dictation books of letters in shorthand in a day at the office and never feel tired at all. The Lord also used me to be a living witness for Him in my home, leading my mother, my elder brother and his wife, and a friend to the Lord."

Chapter Sixty-Seven

Tara
"It costs tears to tear veils."
–Anonymous

Tara moved into our neighborhood in the city of Dhaka. I first met her when she came to church with Judy, whose story you just read. Then I visited her in her home, which was a mud floor garage with a tin roof. It contained a bed of wooden planks, a one-burner portable kerosene stove, two tin plates and a wooden spoon to stir the food in an aluminum pot.

She wore a loose pajama with a long sleeved shirt reaching her knees, and a sheer colorful scarf covering her head. Tara, an infant when her mother died, was being raised by her Muslim father. She appeared shy and difficult to approach.

As a preschooler Tara sat beside the gate of the government passport office with her father who wrote applications for the illiterate. She was taught to enter the building illegally, steal the printed forms which her father then sold along with his services. Stealing included food and clothing. Lying covered up all wrongs.

Tara had always accepted Jesus as a prophet but now she was beginning to understand that He was more than a prophet. After several such visits I prayed with her as she confessed her faith in Jesus. Her father, however, did not respond.

Soon after that, the civil war broke out, creating chaos and lawlessness. One day Tara and her father came running to our house in a frenzy. He told us the story. A group of angry youth came to their door to kidnap Tara. Aware of this Tara ran out the back door while the father tried to convince the boys that she was not at home. She could have been raped and possibly killed.

We hid them in a storeroom for several days until we could contact the Red Cross who transferred the father to a Red Cross refugee camp. They refused to accept unmarried girls so asked if we would keep Tara in our home until another arrangement could be made.

This 16 year old came to live with us just 16 years after our only child, a girl, was stillborn. She was delightful. We discovered she was creative, loved arts and music. She continued to study at our home and eventually passed the required final exam for her high school equivalent diploma. The Red Cross sent a vehicle each day to take her to their office where she could learn skills.

We taught her to use a fork, knife, and spoon, use a western-style shower, shampoo her long black hair, and iron her clothes. Each evening we prayed together and explained the scriptures.

After three months Tara came to me perplexed and said she wanted to go to live with her husband. This came as a shock for I did not know she was married. It had been a secret love affair. The marriage was against her father's wishes and had taken place a year earlier. Her father refused to let her live with the young man.

Her father was now many miles away in a Red cross Refugee camp. We would take Tara to visit him once a month so we suggested we discuss this with him on the next visit. She, however, insisted on leaving immediately to find her husband. There was no way we could restrain her.

That same evening she returned with the handsome youth for introductions. They both called us Aunt and Uncle. A week later they both appeared again but this time Tara was in great distress and her husband told us she refused to eat, was depressed, and would not speak to anyone. She had made many attempts at suicide.

While Calvin talked to the young man I took Tara into another room and it was all I could do to keep her from strangling herself. She had super human strength. After several hours of prayer and talking with the couple we said farewell. There was no doubt an evil spirit had taken control. She had renounced Jesus as Savior, no longer read the Bible, and declared herself a Muslim once more.

We felt we had to inform the father so we went to the camp where he was confined awaiting repatriation. He later escaped from the camp and sought her until he found her and by force took her to a relative where she could live in safety. We went several times a week to see her, took special food, and prayed with her. She refused to eat, and with glaring eyes and a rattling sound in her throat sat in a fixed position day after day.

She became weaker and weaker. We could see the veins vibrating in her neck. We concluded a demon controlled her speech and kept her from swallowing food. With much exhortation and prayer, about a week later, she began to recover and soon was able to go back to the Red Cross office to work. Once more she appeared to believe in Jesus and moved in with us.

Tara accompanied us wherever we went and we were aware that she was followed. It was war time and there was a break down in law and order. We knew we had to get her out of the country soon. We were invited for dinner to the home of a Canadian couple who had adopted two Bengali babies and were planning to return to Canada within a few weeks.

After hearing Tara's story they fell in love with her and offered to sponsor her emigration to Canada. Arrangements were made and Tara today is a citizen of Canada. After graduating from college, she married a Christian man and has two children. Her father now lives in his own apartment nearby.

I will always cherish the memory of the months Tara spent in our home as our daughter.

Chapter Sixty-Eight

Christa Egli
*"The volume of your emptiness
determines the volume of your capacity."*
–T. Tenney

For more than ten years Christa was looking for love, truth, and meaning to life. Born in 1947 in Germany, she was brought up in a Catholic home with a desire to know Jesus. Later on she dropped out of church altogether.

As a trained social-worker, frustrated with society, she became very active in the Women's Liberation Movement. This involved taking part in all kinds of demonstrations and actions against the government, nuclear power, society, and the Pope. In her own words she declared, "I was a fighter woman, radical in all I did."

Eventually she left her job, moved to the countryside and lived together with other people in an alternative lifestyle. They earned a livelihood through a co-op health food store. That was the time when she came across New-Age material including Gurus, Karma, meditation, and reincarnation. It captivated her at first but eventually she felt no release. Trying to find God in herself she became depressed, fearful for her life, and desperate to find a way out.

In 1984 some medium told her and her live-in boyfriend to leave Germany and go to a certain Guru Sai Baba in the South of India. This they did. They wanted to know God and wanted to be obedient to the "voice" they kept hearing inside.

After four months in this holy man's ashram, she felt impressed that they should go to Calcutta and work with Mother Theresa. Somehow in God's mercy, the Holy Spirit gently led them through the jungle of confusion, false religion, lies and strife they both were experiencing.

They attended chapel almost everyday but continued to be confused by a mixture of idols and God. In the mornings as they worked in the "Home of the Destitutes" they became drawn to the poor and wanted to spend their life helping them.

At that time Christa became very ill with a high fever. Someone told her to go to the Assembly of God Hospital in Calcutta. One couple prayed for her in the Name of Jesus which sounded very strange, but left a great impression on her. God did restore her health.

Since their India visa would soon expire they had to leave India. She felt God impressed her to go to Bangladesh which was the closest country. They were warned by many that Bangladesh was a poor country and since it was the monsoon season traveling would be difficult. Still they felt God wanted them to go there.

They had little money and no visa to enter another country. Instead of entering Bangladesh at the western border just 20 miles from Calcutta they decided to try entering from the northern border. It was quite an adventure to travel to Saidpur by train, and the next day by bus to Dhaka, capital of Bangladesh. In retrospect they can see how God protected them.

One day they decided to attend church and found themselves at the Assemblies of God Church. They remembered that name from the Calcutta Hospital. It was June 1985. This was the first time they had attended such a service and were very touched by the love they received in spite of their lifestyle. They were traveling hippies with long flowing hair and dressed in white, plain, loose clothing. They both spoke in broken English, and showed signs of pain and hunger. That day they wandered into our church and into our lives.

I include Christa's description of her experience. "During the time of worship they raised their hands, quite strange...But I was sure they really did know God. We both were impressed by the American pastor, Calvin Olson, who very humbly, took off his shoes before stepping to the platform.

"During that service, God supernaturally poured his love over me. I was overwhelmed that God would love me personally. Sobbing and weeping after ten years of desperation, I found peace. I was 38 years old. My search for love and fulfillment was over.

"A few weeks later, Mr. and Mrs. Olson invited us for supper. They had become like loving parents to us, patient and wise. It was actually their love and dedication to the Lord and to people that convinced my boyfriend to open his heart also to the Lord.

"They asked us if we wanted the baptism of the Holy Spirit. My answer was, 'If it comes from Jesus, I want it.' After supper we knelt down in the dining room and prayed. I received this great infilling of the Holy Spirit along with a greater measure of joy.

"We stayed in Dhaka several months, eager to learn more about God and his word. I was hungry and thirsty for God. He was so real to me, so different from all the other experiences of the past."

After their conversion Christa told her live-in boyfriend they needed to get married. Unwilling to change his lifestyle he refused and they separated. She returned to Germany, attended a Bible School and now works as dean in a Bible School and Retreat Center. We continue contact through e-mail.

Yes, I'm a mother, a grandmother, and even great-grandmother; not the way I expected perhaps, but nevertheless a fulfilling experience. I've shed tears over these my children, nurtured them as babies, guided them as teenagers, counseled them in marriage, held their children in my arms and when Ruma's firstborn died I knew how to comfort her. God gave me children too and one day when I stand with them before the Lord I shall say, "Here am I, and the children the Lord has given me" (Isaiah 8:18).

Cal's Wife

First Christmas in village home

Marian washing clothes in village

Marian helping
neighbor cook

Marian traveling
to a village
on a foot path

Marian baking
bread at the
village oven

Brothers suffering
from malnutrition

Marian with
neighbor's child

Marian visiting
a village home

Marian visiting with a Christian lady during a convention

Marian with a friend of many years - 1991

PART FIVE
The Man I Married

"We ought to thank God for the examples of so many men who were good, even though they were not considered great, or famous. When they die, they leave behind them a fragrance of Christ."

–A. W. Tozer

Chapter Sixty-Nine

Calvin, the Man
*"I will be a fool or a failure for Thee, Lord,
but do not let me <u>fail</u> Thee."*
–J. H. Russell

The awesome, complex man I married first entered my life when I was thirty. From the day we met, God let me know that Calvin had a special ministry and I was to support him in it. When he proposed to me in a jungle in North India he said God would always have first place in his life and I would be second. That set the thermostat for our marriage.

Calvin was a great husband, friend, priest of our home, my counselor, and in some respects, my mentor. His spiritual thermometer became mine. We became one in purpose, focus, and goals but there were differences which in all fairness must be shared.

Personality Differences

Adjustments were not automatic and early in our marriage we suffered many frustrations and disagreements. I was the faster thinker and I would take chances. He was the slower, deeper thinker, and extremely cautious. We both made mistakes and both were often right in judgment. I think the scales balanced.

I was over organized and he had his own organization that no one else could interpret. I dreaded the times he asked me to fetch something from his office with the directions, "It is half way down the pile of letters on the right side of the desk toward the back." But he always knew where everything was. That is, almost always. If he could not find what he needed I was called in "to find it." Very often I did locate it and the scales tipped in my favor.

Calvin could concentrate in the midst of distractions, whether it be a radio blasting, a doorbell ringing, people talking in the same room, or his wife asking a question. I usually preceded every important question with, "Are you listening?" I, on the other hand, could not concentrate unless alone and could do only one thing at a time. I also needed to complete one thing before starting another while Calvin could do several things at the same time.

"You never throw away a receipt or letter" was his slogan. When the file cabinet began to bulge we stored the contents in a cardboard box and started refilling the drawers of the cabinet. Later on when I inherited such boxes I was delighted to contribute most of the material to the recyclers.

We never borrowed money or bought anything without paying cash for it. Later, when credit cards were in vogue Calvin insisted that the bill had to be paid in full the day it arrived. The world had to stop until that was completed.

Whenever we shopped together his constant reminder was, "Do you need it or want it?" If I only "wanted" something I would shop alone. However, since both of us were conservative, the checkbook was easily shared. We never inquired what the other spent or how much he or she paid for any article. The word budget was not in our vocabulary.

It was not our practice to give each other gifts on special days as we usually got what we wanted or needed anytime during the year. Living forty years in a Third World country our wants and needs were less than the average American. Knowing my love for flowers there was usually a plant or "one rose," or a handful of wild flowers delighting me all the time.

When he returned after a long trip and several weeks separation I always had some special surprise for him. Once it was a favorite picture enlarged and framed. After a long 3 months separation I attached a cartoon to the front door of our home. It was a drawing of a couple sitting on a porch swing looking into each other's eyes with this caption, "Why not try the far off place called home?"

Neither one of us were collectors until people started to give us "things." Each had to find a useful place in our lives and serve to remind us of happy times together. We both liked to entertain in our home and divided the work. He talked and I worked. No sympathy, thanks! I loved what I did as much as he loved to talk. This fit in well in the culture in which we lived during most of our married life.

Self-Esteem

Was it personality-shaping at childhood, inherited genes, or unforgettable incidents which developed a low self-esteem in Calvin? He was shorter than his brothers and most of his classmates during the growing up years but gained two inches later while serving in the navy. Unwisely, a grade school teacher commented to the entire class one day that Calvin was a "Pentecostal" which in those days was considered a cult. He learned early there is a price to pay to be a disciple of Christ. His close friends were limited to those of the church he attended.

I recognized this early in our marriage and knew I had to do more than just pray for him. In some practical way I must help him realize his importance in the kingdom of God. It was at this point I switched from the role of a career missionary to that of a supporting missionary wife. There were many times I had to remind myself of this decision. Sometimes I failed.

Chapter Seventy

Servanthood
"The true test of a servant is if he acts like one when he is treated like one."
–Bill Gothard

I recall Calvin's last opportunity to speak to a group of missionaries at the School of Missions (SOM; an Assembly of God orientation program for new candidates and furlough missionaries held each summer in Springfield Missouri). He distributed bookmark size pieces of a towel to each person and spoke on servanthood. I still use part of that towel as a marker in my Bible. Calvin was truly a servant to people, not to things.

There were times when I knew I could not eat what was served me. Calvin came to my rescue. He ate the fish head for me and chose the banana leaf to eat off of while I got to eat off the one plate in the host's home. I'll never forget the time we were served rancid goat milk in a common cup. Knowing this would be difficult for me, he drank "the whole thing."

He was approachable because he lived pretty much on the level of the people he wanted to help. Our home was comfortable for visitors with it's bare cement floors, bed sheet curtains, local cane furniture, and unlocked door. There was always a guest room for out of town missionaries or Bangladesh pastors. This offered extended times for fellowship, visiting, mentoring, or counseling.

He was always available. Adjusting to the Asian's use of "time" was not as difficult for Calvin as for me. I felt every minute must be filled with profitable activity that could be labeled and filed at the end of the day. Calvin on the other hand would sit for hours and listen and talk with someone if he felt there was spiritual value. He welcomed interruptions.

We were available any time of the day or even at night in emergencies. Next to his office was a smaller room used for prayer. A familiar scene was Calvin kneeling and praying with one arm around a boy or man and the other reaching out to God. There was always time to pray.

Often Calvin would return late for meals because food was not his priority. If I anticipated this I would plan food that could easily be reheated. Often as guests in a village home we ate cold food in the evening. To conserve fuel, they cooked once a day and did not reheat leftover food. We learned to do the same.

Chapter Seventy-One

Physical Weakness
"Your weakness is attractive to God."
–T. Tenney

Amoebic dysentery was a constant threat to Calvin. A day after I was discharged from a Dhaka Hospital, Calvin was admitted with amoebic dysentery. This meant a week of intravenous treatment.

Boils are common in the country and Calvin had his share. One on his lower back became abscessed and when drained left a hole the size of a quarter. The pain kept him awake at night and bedridden for several days. He never complained.

He also had a bronchial problem that often took him to bed with fever. On one such occasion we called a local doctor who proceeded to take Calvin's temperature with our thermometer. The reading was 102 degrees. The doctor then inquired if this was Fahrenheit or Centigrade. Calvin decided he didn't need a doctor after that.

I was always amazed how Calvin could operate on little sleep, little food, and a body weakened by bronchitis. I have seen him rise up out of a sickbed, preach a sermon in the church and return to bed. Most people were not aware of it.

During one such occasion while living in Dhaka he became weaker and weaker. It was the hottest time of the year and we had no air conditioner. The ceiling fans just distributed the hot air. Breathing became difficult. Something had to be done. Knowing his tendency to feel inadequate, his reluctance to "quit," and hesitancy to draw attention to himself, I realized I had to take matters into my own hands and secretly.

As a woman in a Muslim country I was about to do something that was culturally inappropriate. I went to the government office, requested a travel permit, then to the travel office to buy tickets. This took several days. Then I presented both to Calvin and told him we were going to Malaysia for a complete rest and change of climate. Amazingly, he agreed.

Until his bronchial problem became severe he did not approve of an air conditioner since our neighbors could not afford one. Once while he was away from home I bought a secondhand air conditioner from a Baptist missionary who was returning to the States. It only brought the temperature down to 80 degrees but it removed the annoying humidity, and may have saved his life.

Years later, after fasting 30 days for Albania, Calvin was completely healed of bronchitis.

Chapter Seventy-Two

Confused Guidance
*"No one is worthy to succeed
until he is willing to fail."*
–A. W. Tozer

S ometime after Calvin died I found a paper in his
files labeled in the Bengali language, "Secret,
Personal Events." Only I would be able to read it. It
included a list of wrong decisions he had made in his
life. None of them, as I recall, was very serious but
nevertheless in time proved wrong.

There were times when for fear of making a wrong
decision and with no sure guidance from the Lord he
often hesitated. As a result he would delay making any
decision and then end up making the wrong decision.
He was willing to acknowledge them and write them
down for me to discover. These reveal the human side
of a man who prayed more often and more intensely
than most Christians.

There were times when I disagreed with his decision
but nevertheless accepted it. Other times, however, I
knew his judgment was wrong and I stated my opinion
strong enough to win. Those decisions happened to be
right. There were times he sacrificed his personal
feelings and gave in to the missionary team not wanting

to cause any conflict. Other times, however, he upheld his convictions even though he was misunderstood.

One time that his judgment was not divinely inspired was the occasion of the landlord breaking the lease agreement on the house we were renting in Dhaka, Bangladesh. Calvin's refusal to move because of a valid lease did not work in this case but only enraged the owners. When I started to pack up personal belongings and prepare for the move I was accused of lack of faith in God to intervene on our behalf.

The packing went on and so did the struggle. Finally we were forced to leave within an hour or else our lives would be in danger. In this case, faith in what God could do and what God would do brought confusion. We later learned that such a move was necessary in the many events that led up to purchasing property and establishing a permanent home for the church on that same street.

Chapter Seventy-Three

Fasting
*"The problem of the spiritual life
is not to persuade God but to want God."*
–A. W. Tozer

C alvin would often fast when spending time in prayer for some specific need. One day God called him to an extended fast which turned out to be fifty days. We were living in a village setting in Gopalganj. He not only gave up food but also wife. He entered one of the three rooms of our home and closed the door. No children and now no husband! I was gripped with fear, disappointment, and anger. Living a day's journey from any missionary and the only white person in the village I feared for Calvin's life and for my future.

The account of the fifty day fast, March–April 1963, is written in detail in my diary which I share here.

"March 6 Calvin returned home from several weeks in village ministries, weary and sick. He had been fasting three days, taking no food or water and this was the hottest time of the year.

"He looked forward to the daily shower which is refreshing to his warm parched body. He is finding it difficult to sleep as nerves and muscles in his lower back are tense and painful. Urine is getting darker. Days are getting hotter. We have no electricity and no fans.

"I spend much time with him, reading the Word, praying and fanning. Calvin often asks me to sing and God removes the lump in my throat just in time for the song to come out. He must not know how I feel. Daily we must renew our commitment to serve the Lord no matter what happens.

"I find it difficult to eat. I can hardly drink water when I think of his tongue cleaving to the roof of his mouth. Just before speaking he must rinse his mouth with water but does not swallow a drop.

"Calvin's suffering moves me to tears. He had two showers today for relief but feels God would have him sacrifice the showers also as they add to the dehydration. What discipline! What drives him to prayer and fasting?

"The neighbors are sure he is dying. They don't understand. Accusing thoughts occur more and more as I fear physical and mental collapse. Calvin is reduced to 90 pounds, his skin is drawn over bones. His eyes are sunken in sockets, joints appearing too large for the rest of his body and his stomach is shrunken. His urine is red today. Pressures increase, thirst is causing much discomfort and restlessness. Sleep is difficult.

"Orville and Yvonne Carlson are spending a week with us. Orville is teaching a group of new believers and prospective believers. Calvin, of course, is too weak to attend the meetings. I moved him to the other end of the house so he can hear the music and at times the sound of worship as it comes floating across the canal from the church. At times Calvin and I join in worship in our prayer language. This brings assurance. Positive reports of the meetings adds courage.

"I could not eat at noon. I emptied my heart before the Lord and read from *Streams In The Desert* (a devotional book). The reading for today described the cutting of the diamond for the king's crown. That's what is happening to Calvin. I must not spoil the work by interfering. Again I surrendered my will to the Lord.

"It is stormy this evening. I played the pump organ while the thunder and lightning played outside our home. There is a warning of a cyclone approaching the coast. The storm within seemed greater.

"Calvin no longer takes trips to the bathroom. He talks with me now and doesn't close the door but the fast continues. I pray with him from time to time but cannot stand to look at his thin body, nor can I understand when he speaks with a weakened voice.

"Sunday, April 28. At 10:15 p.m I heard Calvin say, "The fast is broken. God has given the victory." He asked for a drink of water. After a cold shower Calvin relaxed to try to sleep. Every two hours I gave him a drink.

"The next day we consulted the local Muslim physician, regarding Calvin's diet. He advised crushed papaya, broth, jello and salt water. His urine is still very dark. His face radiates with joy. His eyes are bloodshot and sight is poor but that will be corrected soon. Nerves in his back still hurt but we claim supernatural help in his recovery as we did during the fast.

"The road back to normal strength will be long and rugged, but safe, as we claim God's promises. Within a few days two of our missionaries, Orville Carlson and

Ron Peck, arrived at our door. All our personnel had agreed that Calvin should travel to the port city, Chittagong, and be placed under the medical care of Dr. Viggo Olsen of the ABWE mission. This was to be a long strenuous journey of 12 to 18 hours.

"Too weak to walk at the end of the fast, his two colleagues carried him to a small boat where we were paddled to the nearest launch dock, an hour away. After the two hour launch trip we transferred to a train for the long trip to the port city of Chittagong. As I fed him with a spoon during the rugged trip I was reminded that God asks only for submission and obedience, then He takes control.

"We lived in Chittagong for one month in the home of missionary colleagues, Jim and Velma Long, while Calvin regained strength. After a thorough examination Dr. Olsen advised lab tests. Urine and blood samples revealed nothing abnormal. All were amazed that Calvin's strength was returning so quickly and that he was not bothered with diarrhea. To our knowledge there were no ill effects from that fast. I did not do so well on that long trip however for I became infested with head lice that took one month to rid."

Later I found endless notes which he had scribbled on paper during that fast revealing his struggles and victories. This would be the beginning of many fasts though none quite so long or severe. We may not know until heaven the results of fasting but we do know that today there is a group of believers in that town.

Removing the partitions of the three rooms that had been our home for six years, the building now became a church for the growing congregation. A trained national pastor replaced Calvin and we moved on.

Chapter Seventy-Four

As a Spiritual Father
"No man is a success until he has successors."
–A. W. Tozer

I n the country where we served, a son was your "social security." Without a son there would be no one to care for aged parents. Though Calvin never made me feel that I was inadequate as a wife I know there must have been times when he felt the pain of "being childless."

The culture in which we lived considered fathering a son a sign of manhood. I suffered pain because I could not bring relief to his suffering. God in His merciful plan brought sons into Calvin's life. I will mention two.

Freek Van Der Spek

As a child Freek grew up in a Protestant Christian family in the Netherlands. His father used to read the Bible after the evening meals. Freek even attended a Christian school. He went to church twice each Sunday and received catechism lessons.

In 1973 when he was 25 years old, he went to Africa as a volunteer in a Netherlands Government aid program. During that time his life changed much. He was out of the Christian circle and was introduced to many vices through his new associates. This went on for six years.

In 1979 Freek was transferred to Bangladesh to work in a Netherlands Aid program. There he met Mina, a nominal Christian, who was his language school teacher. They were married in December 1980.

After that Mina developed many medical complaints. They went to various doctors, but no one seemed to know what was wrong. One day Mina told Freek that, as a young girl, she was healed through prayer. So they decided to go to a church. Mina's father was working in one of the church related programs at the Assembly of God.

One Sunday they attended the Bengali service which Freek could not understand. In that service the men and women did not sit together. This made him feel very much alone and they soon became discouraged and stopped attending.

By this time they had become aware of the English congregation in the same building, pastored by Calvin. This church was very different. There were less people, men and women sat together, and there the worship service was joyful. It puzzled them however, that people (especially young people) were so serious about Jesus.

On February 29 Freek's father died and they returned to the Netherlands for the funeral. This left him feeling very insecure. When they returned to Dhaka, they continued to attend the church.

On Pentecost Sunday, after Calvin preached, he

invited people to come to the prayer room. This was very new to Freek, but thinking perhaps the pastor would pray for Mina's healing they joined others to pray. They were not prepared for what they saw. The people knelt in a circle, some with bowed heads and others lifting their hands in audible prayers. Feeling uncomfortable they wanted to leave but for some reason remained in a far corner of the room.

At that moment Calvin walked in and went straight to Freek and Mina. He asked them why they had come for prayer. Then something happened which Freek had not planned. The most natural answer would have been to ask prayer for Mina's healing. Much to his surprise he said he wanted Jesus to be in his heart.

Calvin read some verses from the Bible and then prayed. On the way home Freek had a special experience. He suddenly felt that he was another person. He did not want to do the things he used to do. From that time on God began to work in his life.

Every Sunday morning they met with Calvin for private teaching sessions. Later both Freek and Mina would experience the Baptism of the Holy Spirit and the Scriptures would come alive to them.

About a year later they went to the Netherlands and enrolled in a Bible School. After Freek received his B.A. in Bible they returned to Bangladesh to serve as missionaries. He always referred to Calvin as his spiritual father, and in some ways, one who took his natural father's place.

Chapter Seventy-Five

Asa
"My true son in the faith."
–Paul the Apostle, 1 Timothy 1:2

Asa, his parents and two sisters were neighbors, for several years, next to a Christian family of eight who attended the A.G. Church in Dhaka. Gradually, after attending a few functions of the church with their neighbors, they began to ask questions. The father spent many hours with Calvin, alone, and then it happened one day. The revelation of the truth that Jesus is the Son of God and Savior of the world gripped him. He, his wife and two daughters started to attend the church services regularly. But not Asa.

Sometime later we stood beside 17 year old Asa at the bedside of his dying father. He observed the peaceful expression on his father's face and compared it to his own inward struggle to find peace. After the father's Christian funeral, we invited the whole family into our home for several hours where we played the Bible on tape with soft background music and served them food. The Christian love expressed was attractive to Asa but he was not willing to give up his religion.

With no father to support the family, Asa, now a college student, went to work as a teacher in a Christian school where he served for several years. In the meantime the family moved into a Muslim neighborhood. We were able to locate them and would visit the home from time to time. Eventually, however, after frequent contacts with us, he admitted he needed something more than his religion could give.

He had a remarkable conversion, was mentored by Calvin, and enrolled in ICI Bible courses. The whole family now attended the church services and mixed with the Christian community. As we encouraged him to get involved in church activities we soon discovered he had many abilities including fluency in three languages, that would be an asset to the ministry. From time to time Calvin used him as a Sunday school teacher, worship leader, guitarist, and even invited him to speak to small groups.

By now he had completed several courses with ICI (Bible Correspondence School) and his knowledge of the Word had increased. His maturity as a Christian became noticeable to all. The day came when Calvin felt it was time to invite Asa to become his associate pastor.

Then we learned of his interest in Gwen, one of the young girls from the Christian family that was their neighbor in past years. Calvin had the privilege of conducting that wedding. God blessed their home with a daughter Milena, and a son Matthew, who at the writing of this story are teenagers.

Now he succeeds Calvin as pastor of the international congregation in the English language and also serves as Superintendent of the Assemblies of God of Bangladesh.

He traveled to the U.S. to be with Calvin during Calvin's last days on earth, just as Calvin had been with Asa's father during his last breath.

Chapter Seventy-Six

A Difficult Change
*"We must acknowledge the right of God
to control our activities."*
–A. W. Tozer

It happened when we least expected it. In April 1989 the government refused to renew our residential visa. Later a friend was able to copy the original notice in the Bengali language which translated as: "Mr. Olson has been converting too many people and is requested to leave the country in seven days." We could have challenged it or paid a bribe and remained in Bangladesh, but we feared it might endanger the lives of new converts.

This notice from the government and my health problems, seemed reason enough for us to terminate our thirty-five years as resident missionaries. We had developed great friendships with both Christians and Muslims and parting would not be easy. In the future we could enter the country on a tourist visa for visit and ministry. This was a comforting thought.

However, the decision did not come without a struggle. I was recovering from shingles followed by a form of hepatitis, one of the symptoms of which was depression. I knew I could not endure another hot season in the tropics. Calvin did not want to be a quitter. He wanted to retire in Bangladesh and be buried in its soil.

We said farewell to Bangladesh in May 1989 the year we both turned 65. We would continue to serve as missionaries with A.G. Foreign Missions, though residing in Willmar, Minnesota, the town where Calvin was born and lived until he went away to college.

Soon after our return to the States, Delmar Kingsriter, director of the Center for Ministry to Muslims, invited Calvin to join their team. For four years he traveled with either Del Kingsriter, Dale Fagerland, or Ron Peck in ten countries of Africa and parts of Asia. Through seminars, they challenged and trained local pastors to reach out to Muslims in their area. He was reaching far more people than he would had he stayed in Bangladesh. This was a very fulfilling ministry since teaching was one of Calvin's gifts. During these trips I could not accompany him which resulted in long periods of separation, up to five months one time.

Chapter Seventy-Seven

Fasting for Albania
"Fasting is not a handshake to get God's attention."
–Anonymous

I n 1990, six months after we left Bangladesh, Calvin suddenly felt a burden to pray for Albania, a country which for seventy years had been the most isolated communist country. He wrote the following account.

"The following reveals the depth of concern the Holy Spirit has that all people everywhere have the opportunity to hear the Gospel of Jesus Christ. Having worked in Muslim countries for many years, I have felt a concern to pray for Muslims and Muslim nations, especially on Friday which is their main day of payer at the mosque. As for Albania, I had never felt any special burden to pray for them, other than mention them along with many other unreached Muslim nations in a general way.

"In January of 1990 the Holy Spirit began to prepare me for an extended time of fasting and prayer and I sensed that I was not to accept missionary meetings for February and March. The prayer burden, which at first was not clear, came into focus more clearly in February. As the burden for Albania intensified, I began a partial fast with much time given to intercessory prayer for

Albania. There was an awareness that this was to be a very intense time of spiritual warfare that my "flesh" shrank back from. Media reports indicated there was little hope that Albania would go the way of the Eastern European countries that had cast off Communism as there was no viable opposition leadership.

"At first my praying was more perfunctory than inspired. I knew no Albanians, and prayed only out of obedience to the Lord. But soon, the adversary began to manifest his presence. A real struggle began with the principalities that had controlled that nation for over forty-five years and did not want to release their hold.

"The spiritual warfare reached a plane of intensity that could only be met with total fasting (not even water on some days and for a number of nights I could not go to bed or sleep, but continued in the wrestling prayer of Colossians 4:2 day and night). It was a case of being shut up to God in our apartment for the whole month of March.

"At times the darkness of evil seemed to fill the room, and prayer seemed to go no higher than the ceiling. Doubts would come as to whether this struggle would go on longer than I could stand. The whole situation seemed so utterly hopeless. On several of these occasions we called fellow ministers asking for prayer support, as the burden of prayer seemed overwhelming.

"At other times, the glory of God came down and the joy and presence of the Lord lifted my soul. As the end of March drew near, there was a sense that the burden was beginning to lift. Several friends who had been in close contact by phone during this time sensed too that it was time to break the fast. God had heard!

"One night shortly after this, I went to check the apartment door to make sure it was locked. Suddenly the room filled with demon powers. They had come to attack me. It was one of the most frightening experiences of my life. There was an immediate knowledge that these were the principalities that had ruled Albania, and they were angry that their power had been curtailed.

"In fear I began backing up, and tried to call out to my wife to come to help me, but the words wouldn't come out. The Holy Spirit came to my rescue and brought to mind the verse I had been meditating on that day (Luke 10:19), "Behold, I have given you authority to trample on serpents and scorpions, and over all the power of the enemy, and nothing shall by any means hurt you." Suddenly a holy boldness took over, and using the Sword of the Spirit commanded the spirits to leave.

"They then changed their tactics and tempted me to bow down to them. The temptation was one of the most powerful I had ever experienced. But using the Word once again, I told them that I only bow to Him Who is Lord of Lords. Defeated by our Lord, they had to leave.

"Within a few short months changes began to take place in Albania. The door to Albania that had been closed so tightly, finally had opened. Let me hasten to conclude by saying, I do not claim that it was my prayers only, that were responsible for the door opening. Many others had been praying as well. It is important, however, to be faithful in responding to the call to spiritual warfare. Our weapon of prayer is "mighty through God to tearing down Satan's strongholds."

Chapter Seventy-Eight

Bangladesh–The Now Country
"It's amazing what you can accomplish
if yo udo not care who gets the credit."
–Harry S. Truman

O nce more we began to feel a burden for the people of Bangladesh where we had served for 35 years. In 1994 David Grant, Area Director for Southern Asia, invited us to again concentrate our ministry in that field. What a joy to return to that land where our career had suddenly halted three years previously by the government's refusal to grant us a residential visa. This time we returned on a tourist visa with many opportunities for short term ministry.

We now saw the country, the people, and work from a different perspective. And we liked what we saw. We felt rewarded, fulfilled, satisfied, and blessed to be a part of God's program in that land. With this new assignment we were able to engage in training leaders through the Bible School and pastors seminars. This was to become an annual trip for the next ten years ending only when God called Calvin home.

Which blow breaks the stone of a "stone breaker"? I watched men and women, and sometimes children, in Bangladesh sit for hours on a pile of stones or bricks hammering away at one stone at a time until it becomes tiny pebbles to be used as aggregate. Often it would take several blows to make the first break in the large stone. And so it is with making disciples. Who can say which blow brought the sinner to repentance when so many different people had touched their lives.

The Bible is now being read on the government owned radio along with the Muslims Koran and Hindu Gita. The International Correspondence Institute (ICI) is supplying courses to thousands of youth. Permission has been granted by the government controlled television for a weekly children's program. This program, now in the making, will appear in the near future.

In 1972 land was purchased in Dhaka and today a large Church center seating over 1,000 provides space to accommodate ICI (Bible courses by correspondence), and a day school of 600 children, Bible school classrooms and dormitories for training national pastors, audiovisual department and a printing press. Surely NOW is the time for Bangladesh!

We are unprepared for the revival that is happening. There are too few workers. Need we confess like the disciples, "We are not able to draw the net because of the multitude of fishes," while Jesus stands on the shore waiting for us to bring in the fish.

Chapter Seventy-Nine

The Last Days
"You really can't measure a tree
until it's lying down."
–Carl Sandburg wrote this
about Abraham Lincoln

November 15, 1998, we walked into the Willmar church to discover that a special celebration, "Cal Olson Day" had been planned. Calvin was one of the first members of the church. Now after completing 40 years as a missionary, the church wanted to celebrate his life. He was totally surprised and as usual did not know how to handle the personal attention.

They showed a video of Calvin's life from childhood which I had secretly helped them put together. There was a delegation from North Central University which presented him with a gift box containing the mantle for an honorary doctorate. This degree would be presented at the spring commencement services of NCU in Minneapolis. He was invited to be the speaker at the baccalaureate service preceding the commencement.

It was all well done and so appropriate.

In the winter of 1998 Calvin began having digestion problems. This condition worsened and he was advised to see a doctor. Tests showed a growth on the colon and surgery was performed in November of the same year. The report was not good. The cancerous tumor had also effected the lymph glands. Treatment was advised.

For nine months Calvin wore a pump attached to his waist that controlled the flow of chemo into a vein via a port-a-cath implanted just above his heart near the left shoulder. During those treatments he drove many hours to continue ministry. Most people did not know what his suit coat concealed. He never talked about it. Periodic blood tests showed that there was no improvement as the cancer cell count kept rising. Calvin, then decided to terminate the chemo treatments.

Receiving an invitation to speak at the Bangladesh Assemblies of God General Council Calvin made plans for yet another trip to Bangladesh in February 2000.

The thirty-two hour trip by three planes was uncomfortable. After the first week in Bangladesh Calvin's digestive system was shutting down and he took only liquids. The pain in abdomen and chest increased. At the guesthouse in Dhaka there were nights neither of us could sleep. He was rapidly becoming dehydrated. A British doctor staying at the same guesthouse advised us to see the doctor at the British High Commission dispensary.

Upon examination the doctor gave Calvin a large supply of morphine which helped him deliver three of the four scheduled messages at the Convention. One morning I noticed a change in the color of his skin. He was becoming jaundiced. Even though we knew Calvin wanted to die in the country where he had served so many years, still we felt it best we return to the States at once. Within two days we were on our way home. By now he was too weak to walk alone so a wheelchair was provided for the entire trip.

His last visit to Willmar Assembly of God was a memorable one. Sitting on the last pew we glanced at the platform and discovered the President of North Central University, Dr. Gordon Anderson, and their famous choir were to minister in the morning service.

During the service a microphone was brought to Calvin and with all the strength he could muster, he gave his last words of challenge to the congregation and more specifically to the youth, ending with these words. "I now pass the torch to you to carry the Gospel message to places I cannot go."

At the close of the service we were surrounded by people wanting to express their love and appreciation, knowing it could be their last opportunity to do so. As we walked out of the sanctuary, there standing in a semicircle in the foyer, was the NCU choir which burst into singing, "Praise God From Whom All Blessings Flow." What a benediction!

Chapter Eighty

Promotion
*"Rest is simply release. The 'rest' is not
something we do. It is what comes to us
when we cease to do."*
–A. W. Tozer

The doctor at the Mayo Clinic in Rochester, Minnesota, told us what we did not want to hear. The cancer had reached the liver and Calvin had three weeks to live. From then on our thoughts went heavenward as we planned for the inevitable. God chose to relieve Calvin of all further pain and took him home just one month after returning from Bangladesh.

Cal planned his own funeral. He even asked Minnesota Superintendent, Clarence St. John what his schedule was for the next month. He must die at a time convenient to all. He said scheduling the funeral for Saturday would mean people would not have to take off from work.

Also he requested Superintendent St. John not to mention his name as he wanted the memorial service to be a celebration of praise. The choir will sing. There will be drums, bass guitar, piano, and keyboard, and the congregation would sing worship songs.

Forty-eight years ago sitting on opposite ends of a

makeshift platform in a tent meeting in North India, Calvin held his cornet on his lap and I held a song in my throat as we waited our turn to perform. Even before we held a conversation we knew that we had this one thing in common, music.

Calvin is gone now where there is perpetual music. Only one month after I said goodbye to him I joined the church choir where along with others I practice for the day we can join him and the heavenly choir. I am grateful to the music and music makers of our church who have brought healing and hope to me.

There was no traditional committal at the graveside but at the altar of the church. The place where Calvin dedicated his life to serve the Lord many years ago became the very place where we committed him to heaven. I renewed my commitment that day as I read at the memorial service the letter I had written to God.

"Dear Father God, I want to talk to You about one of Your sons, Calvin. I know I was married to a prince and he treated me like a princess. Our love was your wedding gift to us. I knew he was someone special from the very first time we met. I was awed, frightened and challenged when I realized You had chosen us as a team. You let me share his life on earth for 44 years, and now You want him closer to Yourself. How can I say no?

"Thank Your angels for a job well done. They had a difficult assignment during our 35 years in Bangladesh for we both have knocked on Heaven's gates many times and You sent us back to earth to work some more. Like the time I was dying from cholera; the time we were robbed facing two daggers and a machine gun; and during the civil war when bombs fell all around us shaking our house and cracking the window panes; and the time a mob surrounded Calvin calling for his blood.

And You said, "Not yet." But now is the time You have chosen to open Heaven's gate, not for both of us but for Calvin alone. We would have chosen to have gone together.

"Father, I got to know You better because of Calvin. He taught me right priorities and when we decided to marry he informed me that I could not have first place in His life. I agreed knowing You were first but I must admit it was not an easy commitment. You gave us a job to do together. He has finished first but evidently I have more to do. Please speak loudly and clearly to me as I tend not to hear as readily as he, and help me to be obedient and faithful as he was at any cost. Love to you both, Marian."

Phil and Julie came into our lives in 1969 as we began our Dhaka ministry. He and Calvin were prayer partners for many years. A friendship developed that continues with me to this day. I include Phil's tribute.

"How does one pay adequate tribute to a pioneer, a missionary statesman, a mystic, a loving husband, and most importantly to me, my spiritual mentor for the past three decades? Cal was a unique man of God with feet on earth and heart in heaven.

"I reminisce backward through the years, most of which were spent as colleagues in Cal's adopted country, Bangladesh. Cal was to me:

A man of spiritual passion. Cal knew the forces of evil and good as few have. He was called to spiritual warfare. His life of fasting and prayer sometimes challenged the rest of us mortals and sometimes intimidated us. Prayer was breath and life and energy for Cal.

A man of authenticity. Such was Cal's foundation of authentic humility. No pretense. No self exaltation. Just a humble, powerful walk with the Lord that kept him embraced in an attitude of awe that God could ever use such a weak vessel for His honor and glory.

A man of courage. The year 1971 was difficult for the Olsons in Bangladesh during the civil war. Bullets slammed into their residence; robbers with machine gun and daggers attacked them in their home. Repeatedly Cal went into old Dhaka to preach Christ to violent Muslims who at one point stoned his car.

A man of appreciation and grace. A man of relationships. Cal had an uncanny way of drawing people to himself and subsequently to His Lord. Of course, there was no other person in this world as close to Cal as Marian. Actually, I feel Cal kind of worshipped Marian. She was never far from his words, his thoughts, his prayers, or even his side. The inseparable duo.

A man of perseverance. Well, Cal, you made it. Faithful to the end! What a life! What a man."

                                                    –Phil Parshall

---

As we disembarked in Bangladesh, after one sea voyage, the ship's crew stood on deck watching us climb down a rope ladder to a waiting steamer. In the background was 250 square miles of the famous Sundarband jungle, home of approximately 400 Bengal tigers and 30,000 deer. One sailor offered, "You must be crazy to give your life for this."

AND WE WERE CRAZY…BUT as someone stated so well:

> *"I will be a fool or a failure for Thee, Lord,*
> *but do not let me fail Thee.*
> *I would rather be a success in your eyes*
> *and a failure in the eyes of men*
> *Than to be a success in the eyes of men*
> *and a failure in your eyes."*
>
> *–J. Howard Russell*

> *"A scroll of remembrance (diary), was written in His presence concerning those who feared the Lord and honored His name."*
>
> *–Malachi 3:16*

The Man I Married

Calvin with first convert and son

Calvin with music team at convention

Calvin sitting inside village church

Calvin preaching
at baptismal
service

Distributing
rice after
1971 flood

Building houses for
survivors after 1970 tidal
wave that killed one-half
million people

Calvin with
village pastor

Calvin discipling
a new convert

Teaching in a
Bible School

Presenting a
new cycle to a
young pastor

Calvin with
pastors at a
conference

Witnessing to a
Hindu man

Visiting with
a traveling
musician

Praying in a cave at prayer mountain in Korea

Cal's last visit to Willmar church

Cal's last public appearance before his death

Epilogue

Commitment

"I won't look back, let up, slow down, back away or be still.

My past is redeemed, my present makes sense, my future is secure.

My face is set, my gait is fast, my goal is Heaven.

"I won't give up, shut up or let up until I have stayed up,

Prayed up and paid up for the cause of Jesus Christ.

I must go 'til He comes, give 'til I drop, and preach 'til He stops me."

−An African Martyr

A Tribute

Calvin and Marian, we thank you for your obedient service to God. Your passion and love for the lost has had a great influence on our lives. Your love and encouragement has given us the determination to pursue what God has called us to do. Through you, we have found contentment and joy in difficult times. Recalling your perseverance and endurance during stressful situations helped us tremendously during our first year assignment abroad. We learned to be quiet in the face of accusation and innuendo and allowed God to speak for us. As rookie missionaries we offer you the highest appreciation and praise for setting the bar high. "We follow you as you follow Christ."

Stan and Ann Steward
Assemblies of God Missionary Associates

Calvin Olson Scholarship Fund

Profits from the sale of this book will go to the "Calvin Olson Scholarship Fund" which was established by The Assembly of God, Willmar, Minnesota, in 1999. These funds are available for mission-major students only. Already the fund has been used for college tuition and student loans. During his last service in the church before his death on March 8, 2000, Calvin addressed the congregation, speaking to the youth especially, with the following words: "From now on it is up to you to carry the gospel torch into the whole world."

Marian continues to reside in Willmar and is active in the local Assembly of God Church, singing in the choir and participating in their mentoring program. In addition to speaking to women's groups, she keeps in touch with people in many countries through e-mail. She maintains an "open door" policy and entertains visitors from the U.S.A. and abroad. Already she is collecting material for a second book.

National Anthem of Bangladesh

My Bengal of Gold
আমার সোনার বাংলা

আমার সোনার বাংলা, আমি তোমায় ভালোবাসি।

চিরদিন তোমার আকাশ, তোমার বাতাস, আমার প্রাণে বাজায় বাঁশি॥

ও মা, ফাগুনে তোর আমের বনে ঘ্রাণে পাগল করে,

মরি হায়, হায় রে‌‌‌‌‌_____

ও মা, অঘ্রানে তোর ভরা ক্ষেতে আমি কি দেখেছি মধুর হাসি॥

কী শোভা, কী ছায়া গো, কী স্নেহ, কী মায়া গো_____

কী আঁচল বিছায়েছ বটের মূলে নদীর কূলে কূলে।

মা,তোর মুখের বাণী আমার কানে লাগে সুধার মতো,

মরি হায়, হায় রে_____

মা, তোর বদনখানি মলিন হলে, ও মা আমি নয়ন জলে ভাসি॥

My Bengal of gold, I love you
Forever your skies, your air set my heart in tune
     as if it were a flute.
In Spring, Oh mother mine, the fragrance from
     your mango-groves makes me wild with joy–
     Ah, what a thrill!

In Autumn, Oh mother mine,
     in the full-blossomed paddy fields,
I have seen spread all over—sweet smiles!
Ah, what a beauty, what shades, what an affection
     and what a tenderness!
What a quilt have you spread at the feet of
     banyan trees and along the banks of rivers!
Oh mother mine, words from your lips are like
     Nectar to my ears!
     Ah, what a thrill!
If sadness, Oh mother mine, casts a gloom on your face,
     my eyes are filled with tears!

Original in Bengali by Rabindranath Tagore   Translation by Prof. Syed Ali Ahsan